English Style

Laurie Jo Green

English Style

BY SUZANNE SLESIN
& STAFFORD CLIFF
PHOTOGRAPHS BY KEN KIRKWOOD

Foreword by Terence Conran
Preface by Fiona MacCarthy
Design by Stafford Cliff

Research Associate, Lesley Astaire

Clarkson N. Potter, Inc./Publishers

DISTRIBUTED BY CROWN PUBLISHERS, INC. NEW YORK

TO MICHAEL AND JAKE
STEINBERG
ARTHUR AND GLADYS
CLIFF

Published by Clarkson N. Potter, Inc.,
One Park Avenue, New York,
New York 10016, and simultaneously
in Canada by General Publishing
Company Limited

Manufactured in Japan

Library of Congress Cataloging in
Publication Data
Slesin, Suzanne.
   English style.
   1. Interior decoration—Great
Britain—History—20th century.
2. Decoration and ornament—Great
Britain—History—20th century.
I. Cliff, Stafford.   II. Title.
NK2043.A1S56   1984
747.22   84-2090
ISBN: 0-517-55276-0
10 9 8 7 6 5 4 3 2

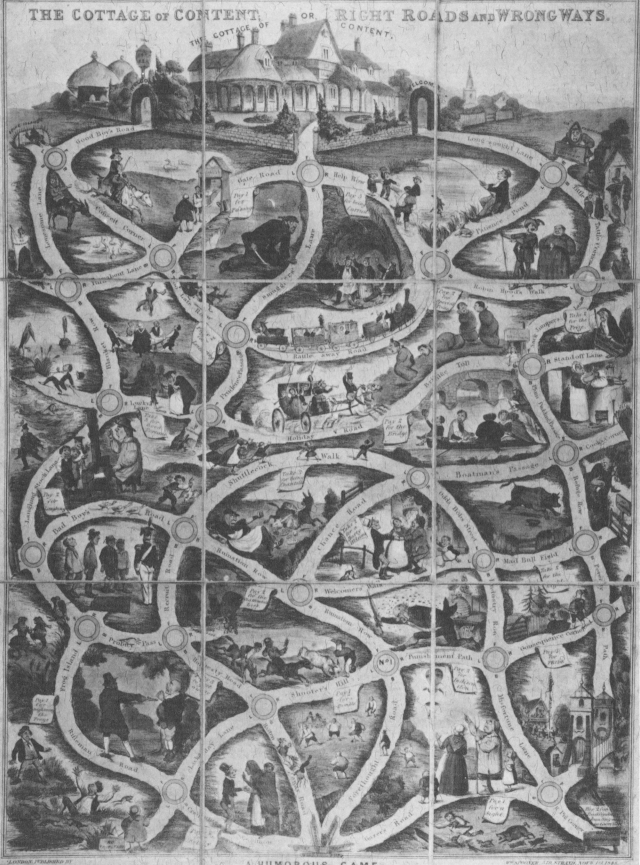

Acknowledgments

We would like to thank all those who allowed us to photograph their homes. It is their design and decorating ideas that make *English Style* such a personal as well as inspirational document.

But we could not have produced *English Style* were it not for the people on both sides of the Atlantic who went out of their way to provide leads, assistance, information, and enthusiastic support.

We are grateful:

● to Debbie Anthony, Zeev Aram, Richard Barker, Stephen Bayley, Sam Blount, Graham Boad, Priscilla Boniface, Judy Brittain, Ken Brozen, Mario Buatta, Antonio and Priscilla Carluccio, Terence and Caroline Conran, Harrison Cultra, Georgina Fairholme, Andrew and Alice Fiske, Michael Formica, Max Gordon, Grayson Hall, Arlene Hirst, Keith and Chippy Irvine, Bill Jacklin, Allen Jones, John Kasmin, Alex Kroll, Michael Lichtenstein, Mary Fox Linton, Andrew Logan, Stephen Long, Rupert Lord, Alain Mertens, Derek Miller, Deirdre Morrow, Tom Parr, Andrew Pettit, Malcolm Riddell, Janet Ruttenberg, Inda Schaenen, Allan A. Schneider, Christopher Smallwood, Gavin Clive-Smith, Penny Sparke, Michael Spice, John Stefanidis, Virginia Storey, Tim Street-Porter, Kathe Telingator, Helen Walker, Rupert and Sally Watts, Piers von Westenholz, and Alyson Wilson. Our special thanks to Terence Conran for the foreword and Fiona MacCarthy who wrote the preface.

● to Mary Gilliatt and Michael Boys, whose book on English interiors first set such high standards in 1967.

● to our agent Lucy Kroll; our research assistant, Lesley Astaire; Rosi Levai, who compiled the american catalogue; Wendy Sclight, who provided editorial advice; Leyland Gomez, who consulted on the typography; Ian Hammond, who did the artwork; calligrapher Robert Purvis; Andrew Davidson, who drew the illustration on page vi; Antoine Bootz, who acted as the photographer's assistant in the United States and took the photographs accompanying the catalogue; Kate Hayward, who typed the manuscript; London Lighting; Margaret Kirkwood, who coordinated the photographic schedule; and John Scott, who kept everyone in line. The photographs of the dollhouses are by courtesy of the Victoria and Albert Museum. The processing of more than 5,000 photographs was expertly and efficiently done by Neil Angel, Reg Prince, and Claude Marie at One Stop Laboratories in London.

● to our photographer Ken Kirkwood, whose keen eye and endless enthusiasm made this project a reality.

● to our publishers and the staff at Clarkson N. Potter, Inc., who include Carol Southern, Michael Fragnito, Gael Dillon, Lynne Arany, Teresa Nicholas, Ann Cahn, Carla Lesh, and particularly our editor, Nancy Novogrod. We continue to appreciate their advice, patience, and understanding.

Suzanne Slesin, New York
Stafford Cliff, London
April 1984

Contents

Foreword

Analyzing English style is as difficult as grabbing an octopus, and it has just about as many tentacles. One moment you think of it as something immensely grand and formal echoing our lost empires, the next, something comfortable, informal, and rather down at the heel. And then a stylish surprise, a terrifically elegant modern room with all the perfection and attention to detail that only the best designers can achieve.

We certainly don't have the booming profusion of skilled interior decorators that seem to pervade America, turning dull, little rooms into theatrical boudoirs—indeed, the whole idea of employing a decorator to help "do up" your house is considered rather "nouveau" and something that only the very rich with huge houses or the very unconfident would ever dream of doing.

No, we make do and mend and rather prefer our rooms to have that lived-in cozy look that is achieved by a lack of planning and years of accretion of objects. In fashion, it might be called the layered look!

But underneath the best of it there is a simplicity and stylishness that is particularly English. Never would we overdecorate, overgild, or overpattern in the same way as, say, the French. It isn't really within the contemporary English character to show off and pretend you are wealthier than you are; indeed, the richer you are, the more demure the external manifestations of your wealth often become. The English like their houses to look rather shabby and worn, and this might be considered to be rather pretentious in itself.

One of the clues to English style comes from our maritime inheritance. We were the great travelers and traders of the world, and wherever we went we brought back artifacts and influences: the classical styles of Italy, Greece, and Egypt; the Oriental influences of China and Japan, and, of course, India. The trade was in both directions, and curiously the products made abroad for our own market bearing the influences of a local style seem to settle back into England again and become an integral part of English style— including Chippendale chinoiserie, Willow Pattern china, and paisley fabrics.

Terence Conran

This passion for new imported ethnic products reached such a pitch in Victorian times that it threatened to obliterate entirely the Englishness of our own style. Thank goodness this gluttony received a jolt in the early part of the 20th century when the Arts and Crafts movement, combined with the influences of Charles Rennie Mackintosh, Voysey, Jungstyl, the Wiener Werkstädtte, and the Bauhaus, helped to bring us back to simplicity and a stylish understatement.

This, I think, was a rather good and unnoticed period in English design and decoration, best encapsulated in the interiors of some of our ocean liners and hotels, spreading inevitably to houses and the new machines for living—flats. It seemed to be the first time since the Middle Ages, when we really drew on our own invention to produce a style that was more our own rather than a distillation of foreign ideas.

Of course, it coincided with the beginning of rapid transport and communication, so the ideas spread rapidly all over the Western world. I often think that the designs for many of New York's great skyscrapers must have been conceived aboard an English ocean liner.

Conversely, for at least the last two centuries, the insides of English country houses and cottages have hardly changed. Simple, comfortable furniture—oak and painted pine, pretty sprigged and rosy fabrics, patterned rugs and carpets, woodsmoke, a gleam of silver or brass, all help camouflage and deflect the mud and the pets.

When living in a foreign field, many an Englishman would long for this vision of country comfort. It is a sort of undemanding, uncommitted look that never surprises but always satisfies, and it is practically impossible to achieve anywhere else than in the English countryside.

In the world we live in today, with satellites making everything visible, available anywhere, immediately, it is much more difficult to isolate an indigenous style, but I think there is still an underlying simplicity and understatement, combined with comfort and pleasure in the eclectic, that make the English style instantly recognizable.

Terence Conran is the founder and chairman of Habitat, a chain of home-furnishings stores in Europe, Japan, and the United States. Among his numerous other accomplishments, he is the author of The House Book, The Bed and Bath Book, *and* The Kitchen Book.

Preface — The Englishman's Chair: English

———Hermann Muthesius, the German architectural expert sent to England in the early 1900s to research his massive study of *Das Englische Haus,* was overcome with wonder not only at the architectural style he found evolving, at the kind of house progressive Englishmen then chose to live in, but also at the special sort of chairs the English sat in: those ubiquitous large armchairs described by Herr Muthesius as "conducive to intimate chats." The English love of comfort, their genius at creating a domestic atmosphere of relaxed conviviality (of which the English armchair is an almost perfect symbol), should never be forgotten when considering the three main tendencies of English style this century, those elements that can, I think, be best described as *classical, vernacular,* and *English visionary.* The English-armchair outlook, the quite logical result of our particular class structure and our way of education, is both curious and potent—and, one could argue, it explains an awful lot.

———The 20th-century *classical style,* which arose in a gentle and a very English form in the pre-1914 period, was, in fact, almost a re-creation of the 18th-century *style anglais,* with its reticence and lightness, its charm and common sense, its consistent admiration for the values of Sheraton and Chippendale (resulting in a minor reproduction industry), its rediscovery of English chintzes. This was a style that really started in the country, at a time when social pressures encouraged English landowners to build more modestly, a need answered so immaculately by the neoclassic houses of such architects as Ernest Newton and Guy Dawber, masters of English gentle-

manly understatement. It was a style that in the hands of the famous London decorators of the 1930s—John Hill of Green & Abbott; Mrs. "Dolly" Mann, who almost reinvented Regency; Syrie Maugham; Lady Colefax and John Fowler—became freer, more flamboyant, and, in a sense, more urban. Although the 1930s purists deprecated it, and in the 1950s the newly formed Council of Industrial Design (founded to raise the standards of design in British industry) tried to pretend it did not in fact exist, it has proved a style of extraordinary staying power, of which the obvious postwar exemplar is David Hicks. It is the basis from which the leading decorators of the current period—David Mlinaric, John Stefanidis, and others working in their idiom—have evolved their own new form of decoration, English Eclectic being how one might define it, which manages by some peculiar quirk of English character to be simultaneously formal and relaxed.

———Alongside English classical, another mainstream movement in British design surfaced, in some ways its antithesis. This is the element that I have called *vernacular,* the tendency Sir Osbert Lancaster, cartoonist and supreme chronicler of English styles, has labeled "Cultured Cottage," a style related to but not to be confused with "Greenery Yallery" or "Art Nouveau." It was a style arrived at in idealistic circles at the end of the last century, where the thinking had been influenced by Ruskin and by Morris and where the major concepts—Simple Life, Back to the Land, Communion with Nature—sought expression in a plain and basic form of furnishing: scrubbed oak tables, rush-seated chairs, reduction to essentials. Both in their ideals and in the aesthetic expression that these found, there is an obvious parallel between the English Arts and Crafts Movement and the Shakers in America: indeed Shaker chairs and ladderback chairs made by Ernest Gimson, English Arts and Crafts designer, are uncannily alike. It is interesting how a style of decoration that developed as a protest against commercialism was quickly taken over itself as a commodity readily marketable in an environment in which,

Style in the 20th Century — Fiona MacCarthy

ever since the industrial revolution, nostalgia for peasant life and what were seen as unsullied rural values have been passionate. Vernacular interiors, first marketed by Heal's and Liberty's in London in the later 19th century, reached their height of popularity—with Habitat's assistance and with that of Laura Ashley—in the middle 1970s. The craft revival of the past decade, with the burgeoning of small workshops throughout England, has given the vernacular an added force.

Perhaps the most fascinating part of English style, because the least expected, is the *visionary* factor. Those accustomed to thinking of English style as settled and solid, perhaps a little humdrum, may tend to disbelieve me. I assure you it is there. There is in English life a quite definite regard for and cultivation of the waywardly artistic, the theatrical, poetic, qualities that have had influence on all the English styles of decoration one can think of, from Tudor, Jacobean, Gothic onward. In the 20th century, the work of Charles Rennie Mackintosh is the prime example (though it should, strictly speaking, be defined as *style écossais*): His interiors have more to do with art than decoration. Baillie Scott, as well, worked in a visionary style of medievalist romantic; for the Crown Princess Maria of Rumania, for instance, he constructed an Art Nouveau dream tree house, built high in the pine forests and known as Le Nid. The Omega Workshops, which Roger Fry founded in 1913 with Duncan Grant and Vanessa Bell, were wonderfully visionary in their wide conception of furnishing-as-politics, in fusing art with life. The visionary trend of the 1930s period—surrealism mingled with the yen for the baroque—survived, a little watered down perhaps, into the 1950s when even the influence of Scandinavia, so strong in England at that time, did not extinguish it. It is a tendency that has flourished again recently, not just in intense interest in surface decoration but also in the spiritual possibilities of decor: mobility, theatricality, and wit.

English classical, English vernacular and visionary: Where is *English rational?* the reader may well ask. It is my belief that the rational, although it has made forays into England, mainly in the 1930s, is not a fundamentally English style at all (a suspicion underlined by the fact that Eileen Gray, the high priestess of modernism, born in Ireland of Scots lineage, chose to live and work in Paris). English style is in its essence more emotional than rational, as Lutyens, the greatest English stylist, understood so well. Its antecedents are feudal and romantic, and it is still, in the middle 1980s, remarkably attuned to the great houses of the land, to ideals of English life, which Clive Aslet has described so perspicaciously in his recent study, *The Last Country Houses,* published by Yale in 1982. English style is a part of our imaginative life, inspired by our perceptions both of the real houses and the life we feel was lived there and maybe even more by our fictional buildings, by the great houses that appear in our great novels.

What other country has produced a book like Evelyn Waugh's *Brideshead Revisited,* in which the hero is a (very English) house?

Fiona MacCarthy is a writer and a leading commentator on design. She was formerly the design correspondent for The Manchester Guardian *and now writes on a regular basis for* The London Times. *She is the author of many books, including* British Design: A Visual History 1880–1980.

Introduction

There are those for whom the quintessential English interior will always be the grand country house with its enticing clutter, its well-worn upholstery, and its enviable patina of time. These are the rooms that result from years, if not centuries, of accumulation; layer upon layer of heirlooms; and mementos collected from a family's myriad experiences and travels abroad. These interiors can be read as if perusing a novel, with the objects representing multifaceted characters whose different roles contribute to the history of a room, even though they may be of little current significance on their own.

The English country house style owes its success both to its lack of artifice and to what the legendary 20th-century English decorator John Fowler termed "pleasing decay." Indeed, Fowler's gift has been described as an ability to re-create romantic interiors that have an uncontrived, lived-in look. That sense of feeling secure and comfortable with the way the passage of time affects the surfaces and furnishing of a room is a hallmark of the English interior.

"While American interiors are often designed to provide an idealized picture of their owner's circumstances," said John Richardson, the writer and critic, in an article entitled "The Englishness of the English Country Look," "English interiors tend to tell the truth about the people who live in them." That truth encompasses an ideal goal in decorating—a search for a well-heeled anonymity, a sense of continuity, and a style that is traditional and as hard to define as it is eccentric.

In a phrase that may typically sacrifice truth for effect, but that could describe the appealing eccentricity of many English homes, the 19th-century wit Oscar Wilde said: "Only the great masters of style ever succeed in being obscure." The individuals who create these personal interiors are the freest of designers. They do not rebel against existing conventions because they are simply not tied to them. That may be one of the reasons why even established contemporary interior designers in England today manage to keep their interiors from looking as if they were all out of a single mold.

England has always been a country of individual houses and well-tended gardens, where privacy and a sense of self-containment are important elements. The urban building booms of the early part of this century, which produced the rows of Victorian terrace houses, have furnished city dwellers with thousands of one-family residences.

Many visitors to English cities can't fail to notice the rows of identical houses that line residential streets. The rhythmic repetition of these small-scaled buildings presents a comforting and secure scene. Indeed, one of the principal features of the English life-style is its uniformity. The

TOP: *The long avenue of trees is a graceful introduction to a stately country house.*

ABOVE: *The romanticism of a country cottage is enhanced by the roses encircling its door.*

polished brass knocker on the front door, the cozy morning room, and the neat garden are all components of a style that has become synonymous with the urban middle class.

For decades, the English middle-class interior was dominated by what has been called "the three-piece suite mentality." The chunky sofa and two easy chairs in dark nubby matching fabric were considered the most important and enduring of furnishings for the home. Even if the pieces were set apart in the parlor or sitting room and used only when company came to call—while the family spent most of its time clustered around the pine table in the kitchen—they were essential symbols of domestic solidity.

There were few high-rise buildings in England until after World War II. Large-scale apartment buildings, although less rare, are still far from being commonplace. It is these solidly built structures that in recent years have been divided into smaller units, which provide many of the flats that are typical of the English urban scene. And new and smaller versions of the stone and brick Victorian house, complete with idiosyncratic details, are still being constructed because of the English attachment to the friendliness of this type of house.

In the last few years, however, the public has been exposed to a wider range of styles. A major and enduring influence has been the one presented by the Habitat home furnishings stores, offering a mix of clean, well-designed, and functional furniture. And Laura Ashley, with its small-scale prints and its romantic sense of the past, has also been closely identified with an important facet of the contemporary English interior.

"It's a form of escapism, a town style that imitates the country," explained Penny Sparke, a lecturer in the history of design at the Royal College of Art, "and although the popularity of the style has to do with the fact that it suits the Victorian houses that are currently being renovated, it is a style that has no real roots."

Being part of history and embracing a certain continuity are very English traits. The English have confidence in their past and both know and accept where they came from. But Sparke is correct in noting that the aficionados of this new Victoriana are harking back to a past and a place that may not have existed for them at all. The life-styles presented by these stores have also established new standards and new points of reference, a decorating basis from which people can find their own self-expression.

Since the late 1960s, David Hicks, the interior decorator, has been responsible for the creation of a sophisticated style based on the juxtaposition of geometric patterns that has become synonymous with the urban town-house look. It is a style that is an adroit stepping-stone between a traditional point of view and a modern sensibility.

Maybe more important, the cultural revolution of the 1960s brought with it the Beatles, Pop imagery, and instant decorating gratification. The look of a room and its high styling became all important. Cardboard and inflatable furniture, bold graphics and dramatic lighting, were the preferred choice of the young and upwardly mobile.

While it was the English design scene of the 1960s—with its loud and startling graphics, untraditional attitudes, and revolutionary ideas that were so influential on an international level—it is the calmer and more romantic English country house look in its various guises that has been over the last few years one of the country's most exportable interior design commodities, especially in the United States. The rose-covered cottages, the dressers filled with blue and white china, the comfortable sofas upholstered in blowsy faded chintz, the scrubbed pine kitchen tables, are all decorating elements that promise an instant pedigree and have been adapted in part because of this appeal.

Those who think of the contemporary expression of English style as either predominantly traditional or graphically modern may be surprised by the current trend in interior decoration. It is an eminently pleasant style, starker, often monochromatic, and more personal than that associated with the strident 1960s, and one that mixes the objects of different periods and relies more on emphasizing the silhouettes and textures of furnishings than on juxtaposing patterns. And in a country where overcast skies are a cliché born of experience, white walls, with their ability to reflect light, have become an accepted part of the decorating vernacular.

The approach involves a synthesis of both old and new design values and emphasizes permanence and quality. A simple thatch cottage is preserved and modernized. The well-worn stone on many back-door steps, where generations of cooks and housekeepers sharpened the kitchen knives, and the functional wooden latches that adorn the doors of rustic cottages are time-honored elements that rather than being eliminated are steadfastly guarded as important punctuation marks.

The conversion of factory and commercial loft buildings into residential units and the ensuing openness of this high-tech aesthetic is the most recent development. Loft living has come rather late to Britain, in part because the lack of housing was not an impetus, but also because of the basic English affinity for conservativism. In London, lofts are located in areas that do not, a priori, have the small-town neighborhood facilities and the neighbors that are deemed necessary to many English city dwellers.

English style today is a synthesis of various tendencies that reach back into the country's history and culture. Its contemporary interpretation not only respects the past but also seems to be in the process of presenting a new kind of pared-down image that is more in keeping with the 1980s. It is, not surprisingly, a rather understated design message. For, all of its diversity of expression, English style, in all of its guises, is most of all a livable style.

ENGLISH CLASSICS

Hunting parties on country estates, teas in wood-paneled libraries, cozy weekends in bucolic picture postcard thatch cottages set among colorful perennial flower gardens, all these idyllic and typically British scenes exist in both fiction and reality and all convey a sense of comfort, intimacy, and continuity. Classic English surroundings seem to embody almost everyone's idea of home. And while these can range from the outlandish and marvelously frivolous, as seen in a Tudor-style tree-house folly, to the particular kind of British understatement that is exemplified in a modernistic house of the 1930s, British classics have managed not to become clichés. Although pleasantly familiar, they retain an individuality that is a hallmark of their continued vitality.

The articulated roofscape is part of Felbrigg Hall. an early 17th-century Jacobean mansion in Norfolk, now a property of the National Trust.

Dollhouse in the modernistic style of the 1920s and 1930s.

VINTAGE VICTORIAN TERRACE HOUSE

The house at 18 Stafford Terrace, near London's Kensington High Street, is a rarity among rarities—a Victorian interior virtually untouched since Edward Linley Sambourne and his wife, Mary Ann, moved there in 1874. Sambourne, a cartoonist for *Punch* magazine, lived in the house until he died in 1910. His two children grew up there and his son, Roy, a bachelor, remained there all his life. At his death in 1946, the house was left to Roy Sambourne's married sister, who subsequently bequeathed it to her daughter, the Countess of Rosse.

In 1958, the countess founded the Victorian Society in the house's morning room. In 1980, after her husband's death, she sold the building to the Greater London Council. It is currently responsible for the day-to-day operation of 18 Stafford Terrace, which is open to the public on Wednesdays and Sundays.

Entering the four-floor structure, one begins to slip back in time. From the stained-glass windows in the dining room and the fountain on the landing, to the still intact William Morris wallpaper and the L-shaped drawing room with its two fireplaces and the myriad knickknacks and ornaments, to the hardware on the sink in the ground-floor lavatory, one has the opportunity to witness firsthand the

diversity and richness of the typical Victorian interior. Sambourne's diaries, picture files, and artist's tools and materials as well as his leather-bound volumes of *Punch* add to the house a dimension of poetry and an intensely romantic aura.

ABOVE FAR LEFT: *A glass window box is cantilevered out of the bay window in the dining room of the 19th-century house.*

ABOVE CENTER: *The sliding engraved brass plate advised visitors whether Sambourne was at home or absent.*

ABOVE LEFT: *The Victorian house, once the home of Edward Linley Sambourne, is in South Kensington.*

LEFT: *The dining room occupies the front half of the ground floor. The walls are covered with William Morris pomegranate wallpaper, as well as with a collection of china and framed prints and drawings.*

ABOVE: *A small chest holds Sambourne's pens and leather-bound diaries.*

RIGHT: *Chairs and chests have been symmetrically arranged near the bubbling fountain on the stairway landing.*

ABOVE: *The stained-glass window in the morning room has insets in the shape of family crests.*

LEFT: *A mandolin hangs on the wall of the morning room. The wallpaper, a William Morris design, has never been restored.*

RIGHT: *The round convex mirror is capable of reflecting the entire morning room.*

BELOW: *The arrangement of fresh flowers in the drawing room is Victorian in feeling.*

ABOVE FAR LEFT: *Heavy curtains are hung in the entrance to the drawing room.*

ABOVE LEFT AND ABOVE: *The drawing room also served as Sambourne's studio. The artist used the tripod camera for his portraits.*

LEFT AND RIGHT: *The L-shaped drawing room occupies the whole depth and width of the house. The gold ceiling, red-and-gold embossed wallpaper, lamps, overstuffed furniture, ornaments and knickknacks, and ceramics displayed on a high shelf have all been kept intact.*

TOP: *Personal memorabilia cover the walls in what was Roy Sambourne's bedroom.*

LEFT AND ABOVE: *The ground-floor powder room boasts the house's original marble-topped sink and round toilet bowl. The box of toilet tissue is from an old stock discovered in the house.*

ABOVE: *The original decorative brass and porcelain faucets adorn the sink.*

RIGHT: *A collection of prints and photographs fills the corner above the bedroom wash basin.*

A NEW GARDEN PLANTED ON ANCIENT SOIL

The garden at Barnsley House in Gloucestershire had existed inside a protective wall since 1770, but it was in 1960 that Rosemary and David Verey started reorganizing it. "I've been slowly learning a lot about garden history and design," explained Mrs. Verey, who is now also known as a gardening writer and who first came to live on her husband's family estate in 1951.

The four-acre property already had ancient trees and 100-year-old yew and box hedges. Mrs. Verey was influenced by a visit to Villandry in France, and she created a garden that was both luxuriant and formal. An avenue of arched laburnum, traditionally mowed grass paths, a *potager*, and a patterned herb garden are some of her additions.

LEFT: *A flower-filled border was planted by the Cotswolds house, part of which dates from 1697.*

TOP RIGHT: *Pots are filled with plants and flowers near the long 1830 colonnade.*

TOP FAR RIGHT: *The grapevine arbor was inspired by Villandry.*

ABOVE RIGHT: *The late 18th-century classical temple was moved to the garden from a nearby park.*

RIGHT: *A 100-year-old evergreen oak grows near the Gothic summer house that has been in the garden since 1770.*

FAR LEFT: *A long view of the fountain can be seen from the classical temple.*

BELOW FAR LEFT: *A wrought-iron gate set into the 1770 wall opens toward the house.*

CENTER LEFT AND BELOW CENTER LEFT: *The design of the pota-ger, with its walks, was based on 17th-century English gardening books and Villandry.*

LEFT: *Garden benches by Charles Verey are placed along the alley of lime trees.*

BELOW LEFT: *The laburnum walk is one of the more recent plantings.*

RIGHT AND BELOW: *The statue of a hunting lady by Simon Verity, a modern sculptor, is a focal point among the trees.*

TRADITIONAL THATCH-ROOF STONE HOUSE

It is the oldest house in the village on the edge of the Cotswolds in the middle of England. As is typical of the region, the thatch-roof structure whose main part dates from the 15th and 16th centuries is made of stone. For the last seven years the house has been the full-time home of Robert Readman, an architect, who has furnished it with his collection of antiques from the period. "I buy houses to suit my furniture," he explained. "My pieces are simple and early, and I feel that this is the kind of setting that is appropriate for them."

By enlarging windows and removing dark paneling, the architect has altered and brightened the interior. The wood-beamed white-walled rooms are stark and dramatic and usually focused on the furniture—particularly in the master bedroom, which is dominated by a circa 1450 four-poster bed. "It's very special and historic," explained Readman, who now sleeps there with his black Labrador. "It belonged to Lord Stanley who took the crown from Richard III and gave it to Henry Tudor."

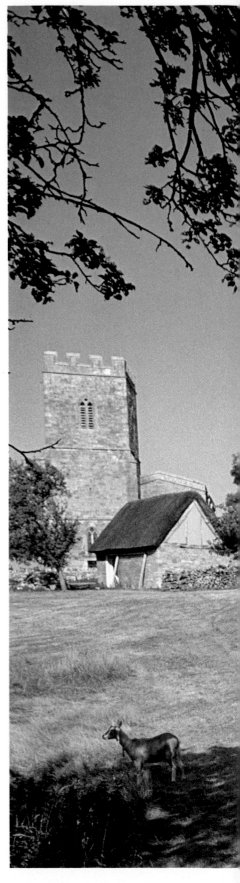

ABOVE LEFT: *Two doorways punctuate the downstairs passageway of the house. The low wood ceiling beams date from the 16th century.*

RIGHT: *The thatch-roof stone house is situated near a 12th-century church.*

LEFT: *A modern Danish woodburning stove was installed in the dining room.*

ABOVE: *Modern fixtures, an Oriental rug, and a beamed ceiling are in one of the bathrooms.*

LEFT: *The upstairs landing with its wooden railing was renovated by the house's previous owner.*

LEFT: *The dining room has been furnished with an 18th-century refectory table and a set of six 17th-century chairs.*

ABOVE: *A French Provincial wardrobe dominates the guest bedroom, which is situated under the pitched roof.*

RIGHT: *The intricately carved mid-15th-century bed that is now in the master bedroom once belonged to Lord Stanley.*

ABOVE: *The entrance to Dennis Severs's house is at the end of a narrow city lane.*

BELOW: *In the hall, the floor has been painted in the manner of the time.*

STAGE SET FOR FAMILY SAGA

The gas lamp and liveried footman are the first hints that one is entering an extraordinary place. "This is the only house in the world that is lived in, cleaned, maintained, and decorated as it was in the 18th and 19th centuries," boasted Dennis Severs of the house where he resides, which is located in an area in London known as Spitalfields. He moved in four years ago with a sleeping bag and started transforming the interior to portray the life and history of four generations of Jervises, a fictitious family of Huguenot silk weavers who lived there from 1724 to 1919.

Three times a week, Mr. Severs leads people on tours through the various times and rooms of the house, which is warmed by ten fires and lit with 100 candles. Each of the rooms—from the 1840 kitchen with its open hearth to the 1760 smoking room with boot-polished floors, to the late 19th-century Dickensian top-floor room with its rumpled bed—is faithful to its day.

"The house is a form of art, a living thing that is not wasting its time with the past," said Severs. There are still lifes that seem to have just toppled out of a painting by William Hogarth; a half-empty glass of wine, an open book, an emotional letter; personal mementos and photographs; and the myriad small details that create the special fabric of daily life.

RIGHT: *A half-finished glass of wine is on the table in the paneled dining room that reflects the earliest time in the history of the house.*

22

ABOVE: *A red-and-gold servant's livery hangs on a dresser.*

ABOVE: *Antique china is stored in a plate rack in the hall.*

ABOVE: *A small table stands on the stenciled first-floor landing.*

ABOVE: *Tall doors frame an antique chair in the ground-floor hall.*

ABOVE: *The late-18th century drawing room is festooned with garlands of nuts.*

ABOVE: *All around the edge of the room is the dried lavender used to sweep the floors.*

ABOVE: *The landing was where guests took the air when the rooms became stuffy.*

ABOVE: *The dresser on the half-stair is arranged with letters, books, and bolts of silk.*

ABOVE: *The Victorian sitting room is on the ground floor. The walls are covered in a bright flowered wallpaper and the pictures are hung at an angle to cut down reflections in the glass.*

LEFT: *The bedroom is meant to date from the second half of the 18th century. Heavy draperies cover the windows. Breakfast is left unfinished on a small table.*

LEFT: *Dried tobacco leaves have been pinned to the wall in the 1760 smoking room. The man of the house would work there as well as take care of his personal toilette. Chairs are hung on the wall; the large chair was designed to accommodate the voluminous hoopskirts of the period.*

LEFT AND RIGHT: *The still life on the mantel looks as if it just came out of the reproduction of the Hogarth painting that has been hung on the wall above.*

FAR LEFT: *The top floor depicts life in the house during the second part of the 19th century. Severs's clothing is hung on pegs on the wall as it would have been at that time. Near the floor are T-shirts that belong to the cat.*

LEFT: *Five people slept in the bed in the top-floor bedroom when the house was divided and its owners took in lodgers at the end of the 19th century. Severs's assistant sleeps in this room now.*

BELOW LEFT: *The top floor bedroom re-creates a Dickensian atmosphere. On the table a cane and bottle mirror the objects in the drawing above the fireplace. A letter from David Copperfield is on the desk by the window.*

RIGHT: *In the late 19th century an entire family would have lived in the single room and used the fireplace for both heating and cooking. The overall color scheme is black and ochre. Severs left the wall as he found it when he moved into the house.*

ABOVE: *Bits of old china fill the dresser that was already in the kitchen when Severs moved in.*

LEFT: *The kitchen looks just as it would have looked about 1840. Severs cooks on the open-hearth stove and lights the basement room with candles.*

ABOVE: *Jugs and bottles are crowded above a small wall-hung cabinet that contains food. There is no electricity at all in the kitchen.*

FANCIFUL TREETOP FOLLY

The tree-house folly dates back at least to 1714, when it appeared on a map of the estate, The Hall, in Pitchford, Shropshire. "Queen Victoria mentioned it in her diary after she was here in 1832 at the age of thirteen," said Caroline Colthurst, who inherited the property in 1972 and now lives there with her husband, Oliver, and her two children.

Unfortunately, the small structure is fragile and can rarely be used. When they were younger, and as a very special treat, the Colthurst children were allowed to have their tea there.

RIGHT AND BELOW: *The early-18th-century tree-house folly has a black-and-white Tudor style exterior and a Gothic detailed interior.*

32

STATELY HOME, MIXED LINEAGE

Although many of England's stately homes have unusual features, Clandon Park at West Clandon, Surrey, is particularly interesting in that it comes from a mixed architectural lineage. The building was originally constructed in the 1640s as the home of the Onslows, but its redesign by Giacomo Leoni, a Venetian architect, in the early 18th century, took it out of the tradition of sedate Georgian residences. A tall two-tone marble hall is one of the grandest of 18th-century Italianate gestures.

Clandon Park has been a property of the National Trust since 1956, and although many of the original furnishings

34

were dispersed over the last 200 years, a bequest of funds, fine 18th-century English furniture, and English, European, and Oriental porcelains have allowed the interior to be refurbished in 18th-century style. The late John Fowler, the renowned interior decorator, undertook the restoration work in the 1960s.

OPPOSITE ABOVE FAR LEFT: *Clandon Park features an Italianate portico.*

OPPOSITE ABOVE LEFT: *The white marble hall contrasts dramatically with the red-brick exterior.*

OPPOSITE LEFT: *The south front of the house.*

ABOVE LEFT: *The moldings and decorative detailing have been highlighted in white.*

ABOVE: *The late-18th-century mantelpiece with its inset oval painting is the decorative focus of the hunting room.*

ABOVE: *The elaborate canopy bed and matching chair in the state bedroom were probably made for Sir Richard Onslow, the father of the first resident of Clandon Park.*

RIGHT: *The library has an ornate mantelpiece, a screen mounted with old photographs, and a glass fish case over the door.*

ABOVE: *A collection of shiny antique brass jelly molds is lined up on the dresser.*

LEFT: *The open hearth is original to the kitchen. On the door is a period rule book for the servants' hall that lists fines for transgressions and gives cleaning directions.*

SIMPLE GEOMETRY ELEGANT REVIVAL

The Cohen house is one of the buildings that was designed by Eric Mendelsohn, the celebrated German Expressionist architect, and Serge Chermayeff, the Russian-born architect, when they worked together in England in 1934. The geometric simplicity of the design, which contributes to its serene and ceremonial exterior, has made it one of the unique houses of the English Art Deco era. The architects also overcame the potential problems that stemmed from the difficult and rather cramped site in the Chelsea area of London, and from the original owner's insistence that an indoor squash court be included.

For the interior, the basic idea, revolutionary at the time, involved creating a series of spaces that were as flexible as they were functional. Doors were hung on hidden tracks so that they could slide out and change the sizes of the different rooms as needed. The spaces flow into one another and the huge windows allow uninterrupted views to the outside.

About 13 years ago, the property was sold to new owners who decided to restore the house to the style in which it was originally conceived, adding their own collection of rare Oriental and Near Eastern pieces to the interior.

ABOVE: *The 1930s white cement house faces its own enclosed town garden.*

RIGHT: *A wide carpeted stairway that is ringed with a gleaming stainless-steel banister fills the center of the house. All the light fixtures are original and have been painstakingly restored. An antique Japanese screen stands in the foyer.*

38

39

LEFT: *The monochromatic living room is simply but comfortably furnished with overscaled pieces upholstered in French linen.*

BELOW LEFT: *A banquette lines the huge bay window. The windows are curtainless so as to allow a full view of the garden.*

RIGHT: *A conservatory, which was added onto the living room in the 1950s, provides a luxuriant tropical garden.*

BELOW: *A long corridor links all the rooms on the ground floor so that full-height doors slide into the walls and allow for a series of flexible spaces.*

RIGHT, FAR RIGHT, AND BELOW
FAR RIGHT: *The book-lined study
is between the living and dining
rooms. Shelves pull out for oversized books.*

BELOW AND BELOW RIGHT: *The
pale sycamore wood paneling and
the chrome hardware, including
door handles and latches, are all
original to the house and have
been carefully restored.*

LEFT AND BELOW LEFT: *The wood-paneled dining room overlooks a squash court, which is located below ground level. The dining table is made up of two sections that can be separated on rotating bases. The chairs have been upholstered in Buffalo hide that is the same color as the walls and floors.*

BELOW: *A swinging door with a porthole window opens onto an all-white efficiency kitchen.*

ABOVE: *The curved headboard, baseboard, and built-in side tables in the bedroom suite were designed by Chermayeff in the 1930s.*

LEFT AND BELOW LEFT: *The hardware in the bathroom also dates from when the house was built. The faucets are set into pale green marble counters. Recessed shelves hold bottles and toiletries.*

RIGHT: *A spectacular antique Japanese screen stands in a corner of the master bedroom.*

HOUSES IN TOWN

It is the London Town of nursery rhyme fame that describes England's most important urban center, which stretches far beyond the financial district of the City of London, as that area is called. From the mid-19th century through the bustling Victorian era, London slowly grew to its present proportions. The boundaries today encompass outlying boroughs, nearby villages, and neighboring towns. There are now parts of the City of London that are entirely Victorian, and characterized by rows of terrace buildings that stretch like colorful dollhouses along the city streets. Often multiples of a single design, they range from the modest "two-up, two-down" houses, with just two tiny rooms on each floor, to the grand town houses that still convey a sense of solid prosperity.

Rows of identical terrace houses are a typical sight in many English cities.

Miniature town house modeled on a mid-19th-century home.

PRACTICAL PLAN FOR A LONDON TOWN HOUSE

That the 1830s London town house was in "execrable shape" did not deter Sir Terence and Lady Conran from embarking on its renovation. Many of the interior walls were removed so as to transform a warren of small rooms into more open spaces.

Sir Terence, the home furnishings entrepreneur, and his wife Caroline Conran, the journalist and cooking expert, have kept the interior of their city residence simple and straightforward. The gracefully proportioned rooms have been furnished with overscale sofas, original Bauhaus designs, early Thonet bentwood pieces, and modern works of art. The uncluttered bedroom and bathroom are predominantly white and, although of modest size, have been designed so as to feel spacious. Many of the materials that cover the floors—from the gray carpeting that unifies the interior, to the linoleum in the kitchen, to the absorbent untreated cork in the bathroom—have been chosen for their ease of maintenance.

Typically well thought out is the duct system that has been installed in the ground-floor kitchen. "In a tiny house, it's important to get the kitchen smells out, because before you know it they're up the stairs," explained Sir Terence.

LEFT: *The hall and dining room take up the front of the ground floor. The burl walnut console is a counterpoint to the modern Italian table. On the wall hangs a piece by the contemporary artist Patrick Caulfield, a gift to Sir Terence on his 50th birthday. The kitchen at the rear can be closed off by folding doors.*

ABOVE RIGHT: *The small and now luxuriant garden behind the house has been completely replanted and redesigned.*

RIGHT: *The recently renovated 1830s town house is the third building from the corner.*

RIGHT: *The suite of 1920s drawings, created for a ballet, is by Natalia Gontcharova, a Russian artist. The chair was designed by Thonet.*

RIGHT: *A hidden duct runs under the shelves in the kitchen to remove cooking odors. The walls are covered with white tiles, pots and pans stand on thick wood shelves, and utensils are suspended from a long chrome bar.*

LEFT: *In the bathroom, a thick glass shelf has been set into the wall. A half-inch slot was cut into the plaster, the sheet of glass inserted into it, and the slot then filled with plaster.*

LEFT: *A tea-sampling box with an image of George Washington that Sir Terence inherited from his Virginian grandmother is one of the objects in the living room.*

RIGHT: *The ceiling beam in the living room shows where a wall was knocked down so as to enlarge the space. The chair by Mies van der Rohe is an original piece; the bentwood side table is by Thonet.*

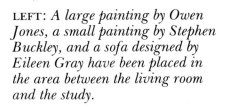

LEFT: *A large painting by Owen Jones, a small painting by Stephen Buckley, and a sofa designed by Eileen Gray have been placed in the area between the living room and the study.*

LEFT: *In the living room, the windows are draped with curtains of fine wool shirting that has been wound around the curtain rods. Old-fashioned cast-iron radiators have been installed in front of the windows. The painting above the overscale sofa is by Richard Smith, a contemporary British artist.*

FAR LEFT: *The use of mirror makes the bathroom look larger than it really is. A long chrome rail extending straight across the room holds towels; the floor is covered with untreated cork that is absorbent and acts like a large bath mat.*

LEFT: *The fireplace in the bedroom had been covered over but has now been restored. "Open chimneys are important for ventilation when you have central heating," explained Sir Terence.*

BELOW: *The bedroom is reflected in the mirrored doors of the built-in storage closet that is adjacent to the bathroom. The Art Deco dressing table was made in the 1930s for an Indian maharani.*

VIEWS FROM ROOM TO ROOM

When Max Clendinning, the well-known London interior designer, decided to renovate the 1890 Victorian house he shares with Ralph Adron, an artist, the designer thought of the way spaces were portrayed in Dutch period paintings. "You could see through from one room to another," Clendinning explained. "And there was always a passageway visible beyond the next room."

Clendinning's goal was to try to expand and diversify the small spaces in his house. "I wanted to create the feeling that comes from breaking up straight lines," he said.

Facing the garden is what the house's occupants call the William Morris Room, an imaginative celebration of the late-19th-century English Aesthetic movement orchestrated by Adron.

BELOW: *The red shutters in the workroom can be seen from the adjoining landing.*

FAR LEFT AND BELOW FAR LEFT:
*The walls in the front sitting room
have been painted in blues and
grays. The house's original fireplace was removed in the 1950s
and, instead of replacing it, Max
Clendinning decided to leave the
hearth open. All the furniture in
the room except for the Italian
Archizoom chair, right, has been
designed by Clendinning.*

RIGHT: *The window that opens
onto the street has been covered
with shutters that keep the room
rather dark during the day. The
painting on the ceiling was
intended to give the low-ceilinged
room an illusion of extra height.*

BELOW: *Clendinning, shown in
his workroom, designed the lamp
and mirror.*

FAR LEFT: *The walls between the kitchen and dining room have been opened up to expand the views between the spaces.*

CENTER LEFT: *A sculpture by Ralph Adron, mounted on a ledge, separates the dining room from the living room.*

LEFT AND BELOW LEFT: *White tiles are the prominent material in the kitchen. The dresser, which once stood in the dining room, was cut down to fit in the narrow kitchen. The wall-hung cabinets have been gradually stepped back.*

BELOW FAR LEFT: *A black plate by Picasso is displayed on the wall-hung serving unit.*

BELOW CENTER LEFT: *Niches hold a number of pieces of glass by the modern Italian designer Ettore Sottsass, Jr.*

RIGHT: *A piece of glass by Sottsass stands on a counter adjacent to the kitchen. Adron painted the textured pattern of the walls and shelves.*

LEFT: *The back sitting room, dedicated to William Morris, reflects Adron's interest in the English Aesthetic movement and the designers of the second half of the 19th century. The ceiling is painted with treelike images and spotted with gold stars, in the spirit of, rather than an exact imitation of, the late 19th century. Adron also designed the light fixture, a fanciful composition made of scraps of plastic tubing, bits of plywood, and papier-mâché.*

ABOVE: *Painted all in white, the room has been sparsely furnished with low comfortable chairs.*

RIGHT: *The interior shapes of the gables and supporting structures on the top floor have been exploited. Access to the room is by a narrow staircase. A small curved balcony overhangs the stairs.*

ROMANTIC ERA FAITHFULLY RECALLED

In the eight years since Bernard Neville bought West House, he has been restoring the historic red-brick building to the way it was originally planned. Philip Webb designed the Chelsea residence in 1868 for G. T. Boyce, the Victorian watercolorist. "This area was a hotbed of artistic and literary activity," Neville said. "The streets around here were buzzing with the Pre-Raphaelites who lived in this part of town."

The lovely wisteria- and mulberry tree-planted garden adds to the unique qualities of the place. West House overlooks the Chelsea Rectory gardens and has the feel of a gracious country house in the center of London.

And, as Neville explained: "Miraculously, all the things I'd collected all my life fit the house like a glove—even down to the William Morris curtains in the exact same pattern as Boyce had." Neville is in the process of furnishing the huge rooms with overscale pieces, many of which came from famous English country houses and clubs.

ABOVE RIGHT AND ABOVE FAR RIGHT: *The red brick house was designed in 1868 by Philip Webb.*

RIGHT: *An octagonal table is set in the center of the breakfast room.*

FAR RIGHT: *The huge drawing room has a wall of 1840 bookcases by Henry Whittaker that came from the Conservative Club. The woven wool tapestry curtains are from Blair Drummond Castle in Scotland. The huge Victorian sofa is one of a pair.*

LEFT: *The dresser in the tiled kitchen holds an everyday service of blue-and-white china. The ladder-back chair is by Ernest Gimson, an English designer of the Arts and Crafts movement.*

BELOW LEFT: *The table and chairs in the dining room were the boardroom furnishings for the Prudential Insurance Company in Perth, Scotland. The Thurston billiard-table lights were made in the 19th century. The 1894 painting on the wall is 16 feet long.*

BELOW: *Textiles by William Morris have been collected and used throughout the house.*

RIGHT, BELOW RIGHT, AND BELOW FAR RIGHT: *The little sitting room that overlooks the garden has a wall covered with English watercolors, mainly of gardens and cottages, including works by Helen Allingham.*

ABOVE: *In the lace-framed alcove of the guest bedroom stands an Art Nouveau satinwood card table.*

RIGHT: *The bed is draped and covered in antique lace.*

ABOVE: *The screen and red-upholstered chair are in a corner of the grand master bedroom.*

LEFT: *The bed in the master bedroom has a canopy of silk plush that came from Mentmore House. The embroidered bedcover dates from the 17th century and the carpet is mid-19th-century English gros point.*

A FRESH LOOK FOR A HOUSE WITH DETAILS

Priscilla Carluccio, a home-furnishings stylist and merchandiser, described the late-19th-century terrace house she and her husband, Antonio, a restaurateur, recently moved to as an "absolutely typical small London house." Situated in South London, near the River Thames, the building is what is known as an end-of-terrace—the first house of a long row of nearly identical buildings. "This used to be an industrial area," Mrs. Carluccio explained, "and the house was probably built for simple artisans rather than for posh Victorians."

While the couple retained all the original Victorian details, including the stained-glass panels over the front door and the ceiling moldings in the sitting room, they undertook a substantial renovation, which included knocking down walls to let additional light into the interior. They also rearranged the ground-floor rooms so that the kitchen faces onto the street and the living room opens onto a small garden at the rear.

ABOVE LEFT: *A traditional Victorian tiled walkway leads up to the front door.*

ABOVE: *A copper pub sign hangs in the foyer. The stained glass over the door is an original detail.*

RIGHT: *In the kitchen, the basket of Boletus Edulis was collected by Antonio Carluccio, an ardent fungi hunter.*

LEFT: *The painting in the dining area is a 1920s portrait of Priscilla Carluccio's grandmother.*

RIGHT: *The kitchen was completely redesigned by the owners, who worked with David Chaloner, an interior designer, and was built by a company that specializes in shop fixtures. The freestanding central storage and work unit was meant to be a cross between a pâtissier's stand and a restaurant display unit. Three stools provide bar-type seating, while saucepans, cooking equipment, and vegetables are stored above and under the counter. The cabinets, with their oval-shaped glass fronts, were custom-made. The floor is covered with German ceramic tiles.*

BELOW: *A small sideboard serves the dining area, which is between the kitchen and the sitting room.*

70

ABOVE: *The walls in the living room have been sprayed with cream gloss paint so as to look like French lacquerwork. The furniture includes two Edwardian armchairs. Sliding doors open onto the small walled garden.*

LEFT: *Two of the objects in the living room are an antique model sailboat and a head carved by Mrs. Carluccio's son, Benjamin Patrick.*

ABOVE AND RIGHT: *The Carluccios and Granby Patrick, another of Mrs. Carluccio's sons, sit in the garden that is adjacent to the living room. The Carluccios use the garden as an extension to the house and eat outside whenever the weather permits.*

73

INTERIOR RICH IN PERSONAL OBJECTS

Stephen Long, a London antiques dealer, perceives the house in which he has lived for the past 18 years as "an Impressionist painting that is being added to all the time." It is an interior that is rich in objects and texture, but most of all in color. "I like strong colors," Long said, "especially yellow and red."

The antiques dealer also likes lots and lots of possessions. "If you have only a few things, they must be really good, but if they're not, you have to crowd them up," explained Long, who was a close friend of the famous decorator John Fowler. So tables are piled high with books, walls are completely covered with paintings and china, and mantelpieces are still lifes in which collections of objects from different eras collide. The faux-marbre surfaces and chintz upholstery typify the interior and richly cluttered style that has been the inspiration for many decorators, both in England and the United States.

ABOVE FAR LEFT, ABOVE LEFT, AND FAR LEFT: *Books line the shelves and objects are crowded on the walls and tables in Stephen Long's drawing room.*

LEFT: *Candlestick lamps with tortoiseshell shades stand on the mantel. The two blanc-de-chine figures reflected in the mirror were an early Long find.*

RIGHT: *An armchair in the sitting room is slip-covered in Old Rose, the late John Fowler's favorite chintz. The curtains are made from an 1825 chintz discovered in an old trunk.*

ABOVE: *In the drawing room, a contemporary copy of a Van Dyke portrait of Charles I is hung on satin sashes over the tortoiseshell-painted fireplace.*

TOP LEFT, CENTER, AND RIGHT: *The clutter of objects includes a collection of boxes made of orange peel turned inside out, faux-bois jugs, ivory bellows, an early example of decalcomania, an Empire basket piled with dried lemons, and an oval tea caddy covered with wax seals. Every inch of the walls,*

including the back of the door, has been covered with a variety of pictures and objects.

ABOVE: *Library busts sit atop the bookcase. A Biedermeier commode and an American Federal painted piece are at either side of a book-laden table.*

LEFT: *The pattern on the walls in the bedroom was copied from an antique screen that belonged to Fowler and was painted onto plain hessian. Bedside tables flank the draped bed with its antique cover.*

LEFT AND BELOW LEFT: *Long started collecting the 19th-century white pottery boot warmers that are lined up on the faux-marbre mantelpiece when he saw a pair used as toothbrush holders by Fowler. The glass is from the 18th century.*

ABOVE: *Paintings on glass are clustered behind a painted chest in a corner of the bedroom.*

RIGHT: *Creamware fills one of the niches in the dining room. The chair, the top of which is just visible, is an Edwin Lutyens design.*

BELOW: *A circular table is set in the dining room, which has two niches on either side of the fireplace. Long prefers to light the room only with candles.*

ABOVE: *A collection of blue-and-white china is displayed on the kitchen mantelpiece.*

RIGHT: *The dresser in the kitchen was original to the house and is now crowded with English blue-and-white china and creamware. Some of the paneling is real, some is painted on the plaster walls in trompe l'oeil.*

RIGHT AND FAR RIGHT: *Barbara Brown in her workroom, which includes knitting, ironing, and steaming areas. Ron Nixon built the primary-colored Rietveld-style unit behind the bed.*

BELOW: *The chest was painted by Ann Martin, an art student.*

BELOW RIGHT: *Each of the cotton sofa cushions has been upholstered in a different color. The rug is one of Nixon's designs.*

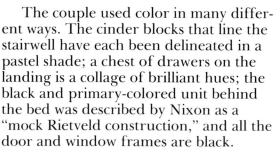

INTENSE HUES, INVENTIVE WAYS

Barbara Brown designs and makes brightly colored knitted clothes, and Ron Nixon creates rugs and wall murals in vivid geometric patterns, so it seemed only natural that the couple would base the interior design of their London house on the inventive and intense use of color that characterizes all their work. Built in 1975, the small house is part of a modern town house complex that overlooks the River Thames.

The couple used color in many different ways. The cinder blocks that line the stairwell have each been delineated in a pastel shade; a chest of drawers on the landing is a collage of brilliant hues; the black and primary-colored unit behind the bed was described by Nixon as a "mock Rietveld construction," and all the door and window frames are black.

"Whenever we want to try something new, we mix the colors up and simply paint over what we had before," said Nixon. "We don't think of this interior as something that is forever."

PASTEL PALETTE FOR CHELSEA HOUSE

Although she has lived in the 100-year-old house for only seven years, this is the second time that Tricia Guild, the well-known fabric designer, has decorated her Chelsea home. "It used to be rather nostalgic," recalled the designer. "Now I wanted to make it much cooler, so I ripped it all apart."

Guild had some walls removed in the bedrooms and in the kitchen to enlarge the rooms and installed a skylight on the top landing. Walls and surfaces were kept to a muted palette. "I planned it all to be very pale," she said, "so that it could act as a background for the things I collect. I like to mix modern and very old objects."

ABOVE: *Traditional stone balconies grace the front of the Chelsea terrace house.*

Included are groupings of ceramics by such contemporary artists as Janice Tchelenko and Carol McNicoll, and drawings by a roster of young artists as well as by such established names as Howard Hodgkin, Ivor Abrahams, and Bill Jacklin. But most enviable are Guild's collections of 1920s and 1930s china and pottery by Clarice Cliff and Susie Cooper.

It is the mix of muted colors and textures that gives the house its special subtlety. Walls are stipled, wallpapered, or covered in fabric, all from Guild's company, Designers Guild. The sitting room is painted in a combination of cream, off-white, pale gray, beige, aqua, and lilac to look, as the designer described it, "like the shell of an egg."

FAR LEFT AND LEFT: *Tricia Guild's signature mix of soft colors, natural materials, and textured surfaces can be seen in the entrance hall and on the landing.*

ABOVE: *A Japanese medicine container and two wooden candlesticks stand on the hall table.*

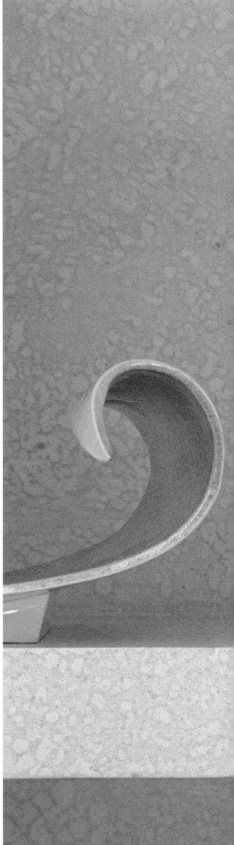

TOP: *The white-and-caramel-hued living room has been furnished with comfortable chairs and sofas.*

ABOVE: *A throw by Kaffe Fassett is draped over an armchair.*

ABOVE: *Ceramics and lacquer boxes are displayed on a small side table in the living room.*

ABOVE: *The flowers in the vase on the trompe l'oeil marble mantel-piece counterpoint those in the painting by Bill Jacklin.*

RIGHT: *A ceramic by Carol McNicoll and green glass bottles form a striking composition.*

86

LEFT: *A collection of Art Deco perfume bottles is displayed on the dressing table that is set in front of the window.*

BELOW: *The closet shelves and curtains are lined in matching fabric.*

RIGHT: *A Designers Guild blue-and-white chintz, called Tea Rose, has been used for the walls as well as the canopy and curtains that surround the lavishly dressed bed.*

BELOW: *A chaise longue has been positioned near the window in the boudoirlike bedroom.*

TOP: *In the basement kitchen, which leads onto the garden, rattan armchairs and a wooden bench surround a pine table. An original 1930s linoleum covers the floor.*

ABOVE: *Guild's flea market and antique shop finds of flower-decorated china by Clarice Cliff and her contemporaries are displayed on open shelves and fill an antique pine sideboard.*

RIGHT: *Well-used stainless steel saucepans hang in front of a patchwork wall of original Victorian tiles.*

SKYLIT STUDIO FOR AN ART DEALER

About 100 years ago, when London's Chelsea area was a center for artists, the row of houses was built as painters' studios. Now, it seems that only art dealers can afford the extravagant spaces.

Three years ago, Roberto Shorto, a dealer, bought the studio that had once belonged to Sir Alfred Munnings, an early 20th-century painter. The huge space was derelict and without a roof. With the help of the interior decorator Geoffrey Bennison, Shorto transformed the studio into an apartment that boasted a 60-foot-long-by-30-foot-high main living area topped with dramatic skylights.

The interior is a play of textures—a multicolored carpet, antique rug-covered armchairs, Persian shawls draped over sofas, and two matching 18th-century French screens. The antique furniture, including a Georgian bookcase and a Chinese export lacquer cupboard, contrasts with modern works by such artists as R. B. Kitaj and Avigdor Arika.

LEFT AND TOP RIGHT: *The main living space is 60 feet long and has 30-foot-high ceilings. Skylights were installed and the pine ceiling was stenciled. The carpet was custom-made in France.*

ABOVE RIGHT AND RIGHT: *China is displayed on a table by one of the armchairs that is covered with a fragment of antique carpet. Small framed modern works of art lean on the mantel.*

CREATIVE WAYS WITH COLOR

When Susan Collier came across the 1702 house in South London, it had been empty for 30 years. The necessary installation of plumbing, electricity, and heating left no extra funds for decorating.

That was just as well, as over the past few years Collier, a textile designer, has filled the paneled rooms of the red-brick Queen Anne building with all of her favorite objects. From the ceramic-laden breakfront in the kitchen to the cool blue-paneled bedroom, in which the bed is covered with sheets from Collier's grandmother's trousseau, the house is warm and personal.

The interior has the relaxed atmosphere that comes from a sure sense of style. Two Afghan ikats keep drafts out of the living room and also act as a backdrop to a table covered with seedpods that Collier has collected.

ABOVE: *The 1702 red-brick house was once occupied by John Francis Bentley, who was the architect of Westminster Cathedral.*

The designer calls the living room, which is festooned with fabrics of her own design, the Bazaar Room. "That allows me to collect anything I want without ever worrying whether it goes with whatever else I have," she explained.

OPPOSITE LEFT: *The back door opens onto the garden. The floor is well-worn slate.*

ABOVE LEFT: *The original paneling in the master bedroom has been repainted a cool blue color. The bed is covered with handmade linen and lace sheets and a quilt sewn from pieces of Liberty fabric. The lace curtains were designed by Jane Booska.*

ABOVE: *The small chest of drawers is a turn-of-the-century English painted piece.*

FAR LEFT: *The barley-sugar banister is a traditional feature of a Queen Anne house.*

LEFT: *The stairs to the basement kitchen were originally used by the house's servants.*

ABOVE: *One of Susan Collier's fabric designs serves as a tablecloth in the kitchen.*

RIGHT: *Collier had once started restoring the kitchen dresser but decided it looked better with the patina of time. The collection of 1920s and 1930s ceramics was bought over the years from her housekeeping money.*

ABOVE: *Some of the fabrics that Collier has designed with her sister, Sarah Campbell, are used for the curtains and the upholstery in the living room. The picture over the* *fireplace was painted by Collier's daughter, Charlotte Herxheimer, when she was 11 years old.*

ABOVE: *A frog-shaped jug by the potter Alison Britton, surrounded by seedpods from all over the world, is the center of a still life of natural objects. Two ikats from Afghanistan act as a backdrop.*

ABOVE: *Favorite creatures such as crocodiles and bugs are displayed on a Malaysian lacquer table in the living room.*

RIGHT: *The inlaid wood and trompe l'oeil table was made by Peter Niczewski.*

FLATS AND APARTMENTS

In the late 19th century, it was customary only for men to live alone. And some of the first residences in London to be built as apartments, or flats, as they are called in England, were probably those in the St. James area meant for bachelors and their personal gentleman's gentleman. But nowadays, the flat has become a typical English urban accommodation. The large town houses have been divided up into apartments, and new structures have been built to meet the needs of those who live and work in cities. Whether a richly ornamented environment that mirrors the occupant's favorite era of the past or a striking modern scheme, the English flat—classical studio, bed-sitter, or dramatic suite of high-ceilinged rooms—is always a distinctly English interpretation of apartment living.

A colonnade lines the façade of a stately building of flats in London's Eaton Square.

Small version of an 1840 South Kensington town house.

MODERN ART IN CENTURY-OLD HOUSE

When the Church of England decided to sell a number of 19th-century houses, John Kasmin became the proprietor of the top three floors of one of the large and solid buildings. The London art dealer not only raised the attic ceiling to allow room for a library and an adjoining roof garden, but also altered the entrance and removed some walls. Although the interior looks fairly simple and rather stark, it was the result of careful deliberation between Kasmin and the architect John Prizeman.

"I'm a fusspot," Kasmin admitted. "I have to have carpets dyed the right color, and am willing to wait to get things the way I want them." That meant special-ordering the heavy pile wool carpeting the color of "the warm brown underside of a field mushroom" that was to be used throughout the house, and mixing the exactly right off-white hue for the walls.

The spectacular stairway is one of the

house's main features. The wrought-iron railing was stripped and the stairs scraped down to their original stone. The rooms are furnished with both antique and contemporary pieces that have been collected over the years, as well as with modern works of art and African sculptures. And where possible, the windows are left uncovered. "Curtains are something I really don't like," Kasmin explained.

FAR LEFT AND ABOVE LEFT: *The restoration of the mid-19th-century stairway included stripping layers of paint off the wrought-iron railing. A cast-bronze hare by Barry Flanagan stands in a niche.*

ABOVE: *All the framed etchings and drawings that line the stairway are by Henri Matisse.*

RIGHT: *A huge turn-of-the-century painted New Guinea Sepik River gable mask hangs by the top-floor landing.*

ABOVE: *A painted relief by the American artist Frank Stella is on the wall behind a table by Jasper Morrison, a young English designer. The table is made from racing-bicycle handlebars, a slab of beech wood, and a glass disc. The African sculpture is from the Cameroons.*

LEFT: *In the living room, an old armchair has been covered in oatmeal-colored linen. Next to it is a 1930s English lamp and behind the chair hangs a 1930 drawing by Joan Miró.*

ABOVE: *Between two windows in the dining room stands an African white face mask atop a French Art Deco cabinet.*

RIGHT: *In the dining room, a set of late-18th-century pear wood chairs surround a modern table by Eero Saarinen. The shallow bowl filled with conch shells is English and carved from a tree trunk. The painting is a 1968 work by the American artist Jules Olitski.*

RIGHT: *A pair of Victorian cane club chairs and a glass-topped coffee table have been carefully positioned in the living room, where a long pine shelf holds a video monitor. The drawings are by David Hockney and Henri Matisse. Simple rattan roller blinds cover the windows.*

LEFT: *A Victorian towel stand, a 19th-century Afghanistan carved wood chair, an early-19th-century English country chest, and a painting by Kenneth Noland are lined up in the guest bedroom.*

LEFT: *The shades on the windows of the master bedroom are dark green, one of John Kasmin's favorite colors. A French Provincial armoire, an original Thonet chair, and an antique Amish quilt complete the furnishings.*

RIGHT: *Kasmin had a fireplace installed in the bedroom as part of the renovation. A Persian vase, an Indian picture, and a small sculpture by his son, Aaron Kasmin, are on the mantel. A Victorian armadillo basket and an Indian brass box sit by the fireplace.*

FAR RIGHT: *The guest bedroom also includes a two-person antique bathtub. The French porcelain taps have been set directly into the wall. The mirror is also French.*

RIGHT: *The spacious bathroom that adjoins the master bedroom was once three rooms. The walls have been painted an eau-de-nil color. The shower stall is large enough so as not to require any curtains. The shelf, stool, and lavatory seat are all of mahogany. The photograph is a Victorian view of the interior of the synagogue in Toledo, Spain.*

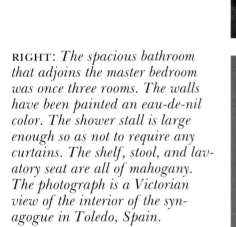

RIGHT: *Shelf-lined stairs lead to the top-floor library.*

ABOVE: *The attic ceiling was lifted to allow the library to be installed under the roof. Doors open out to a small terrace. The walls are covered with photographs of writers by Man Ray.*

RIGHT: *Thick pine shelves that run the length of the room hold books of literature and history. An oak dining table doubles as a desk; the chair is an original bentwood Thonet design.*

SMALL FLAT, LIGHT TOUCH

Shiu Kay Kan, a native of Hong Kong who first came to London in 1969, says his personal style has evolved from "mixing what I've seen in England, Italy, and the United States." His ideas are exemplified in the lighting and furniture that he has designed in recent years, many examples of which he has used in his small apartment.

"It's Post-High-Tech," Kan explained of the simple gray-carpeted interior situated in a Hampstead terrace house in North London. A Japanese mattress, or futon, is used as a bed at night and then rolled up for seating during the day. The storage units, tables, and bed platforms are made from natural-colored industrial wood flats and were designed by Kan and Paul Connell, who studied with John Makepeace, the famous English craftsman.

ABOVE: *Shiu Kay Kan calls his low-voltage halogen-bulb clamp lamp Halo in the Air. Two metal brackets screw onto a tension-strung steel wire.*

ABOVE: *Kan's hanging lamp, called Eco, can be fitted with different bulbs to provide direct or reflected light. His Amsterdam is a remote-controlled standing lamp of extruded aluminum and pressed steel that gives an uplight. The box on the column operates the remote-control dimmer.*

ABOVE FAR LEFT: *Kan's small pied-à-terre is furnished simply but functionally. The storage units, tables, and sofa platform were made from natural-colored wood, often used for warehouse palettes.*

FAR LEFT: *At night, the sofa's wood platform and the low table become the base for a bed in the studio apartment.*

LEFT: *During the day, the futon, a large soft pillow, functions as a sofa. Unrolled, it becomes a flat mattress for sleeping.*

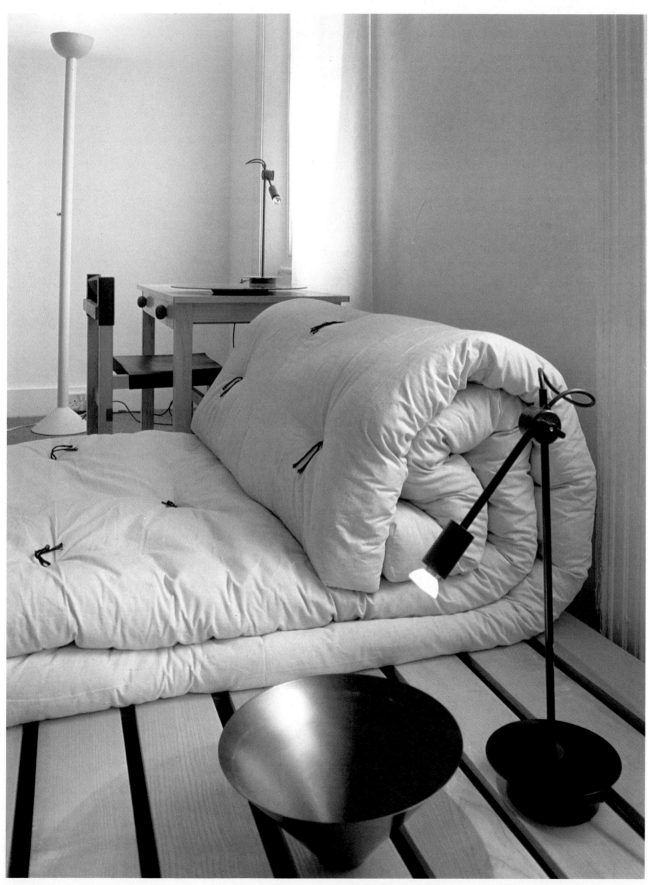

A GOOD MIX-UP OF PERSONAL ANTIQUES

"A good mix-up" is the way Adrienne Barker described the tiny apartment in which she has lived for the last six years. "It's the smallest place I've had, so the things in it are all I've got left," said the antiques dealer who with her partner, Sam Beazley, owns Portmeiron Antiques, a London shop.

Situated in what Barker admitted is "a 1910, ugly but well-built Edwardian house," the tiny apartment is furnished with a mix of idiosyncratic objects. It is a decor that depends on a contrast of rich patterns and textures—a tartan plaid on the table, a 19th-century toile de Jouy on a chair, and two Welsh rugs thrown over the sofa to protect it from the cat.

ABOVE: *In the cozy and feminine mezzanine bedroom, small gilt-framed artworks are grouped on the wall behind the bed.*

RIGHT: *From the mezzanine, one can get a bird's-eye view of the entire living room.*

WELL-CRAFTED NEW KITCHEN

A few years ago Johnny Grey, a young architect, felt he was working on projects that were "too theoretical." They "had nothing to do with how things are made," he explained. So Grey formed a company to produce custom-made furniture and to design interiors. One of his most ambitious projects so far has been the design of a kitchen for a cooking teacher.

The unusual and rather heavy-looking furnishings are examples of Grey's ideas on the traditional crafts and modern design. The primary material for the pieces of furniture is ash wood, with such detailing as granite, glass, and steel.

LEFT: *Sometimes used for demonstrations, the kitchen features a central work counter with a built-in stove top.*

ABOVE RIGHT: *A pot rack and lights are hung over the cook-top unit. The circular red handle opens the built-in waste bin.*

ABOVE FAR RIGHT: *The living room, which is off the kitchen, has been furnished with wicker pieces and matching storage units.*

RIGHT: *Although traditional in feeling, the wood cabinets enclose modern equipment.*

A NEOCLASSIC TOUR DE FORCE

Philip Hewat-Jaboor is a man with definite tastes. "I'm a Neoclassical fiend. I like off-beat colors, sculpture on top of bookcases, eating surrounded by books, and more than a bit of space," said the art and antiques dealer who also owns Hatfield's, a metalwork restoration firm that was established in 1834.

Hewat-Jaboor's residence, on the ground floor of a house that overlooks one of London's loveliest 19th-century squares, is exactly what he had in mind. "I prefer eccentric spaces," Hewat-Jaboor said of the two reception rooms: a sitting room with 14-foot ceilings and an adjacent library that doubles as a dining room.

He has furnished his dramatically sparse living room with only a pair of overscaled sofas, two carved Coadestone sculptures, and a huge modern photograph by Gerald Incandela. "I hate clutter and am not partial to all that awful English mess," he explained.

The deep blue-colored library is lined with bookcases and has a chandelier lit with real candles. "Chairs are a perennial problem," Hewat-Jaboor added. "I will probably end up with stools."

LEFT: *Two large sofas are the room's only seating. Lighting spots are set into the ceiling.*

BELOW: *The high-ceilinged living room is minimally furnished. The windows are shuttered and curtainless, the floors uncarpeted, and the walls are plastered, polished, and glazed to look like suede.*

LEFT: *A modern photographic work by Gerald Incandela is hung in the living room, above the boldly upholstered sofa.*

RIGHT AND BELOW RIGHT: *The library has two sets of tall doors. One opens onto the living room, the other onto the small efficiency kitchen. The bookshelves are edged in mirror.*

FAR RIGHT: *Double doors with brass hardware separate the living room from the library.*

BELOW FAR RIGHT: *In a corner of the library, an Italian modern floor lamp stands behind an antique chair with a monogrammed seat.*

BELOW: *The library is also the dining room. The early-19th-century ram's head chandelier boasts real candles.*

FAR LEFT AND LEFT: *The luxurious bathroom has been outfitted in marble.*

ABOVE LEFT: *The kitchen, with its unadorned cabinetry, is designed to convey a sense of Japanese simplicity.*

ABOVE: *The narrow hallway that leads from the living room to the bedroom links a series of tightly enclosed spaces.*

RIGHT: *In contrast to the living room, the bedroom is intentionally dark and enclosed. The bedcover is suede and, like the walls and carpeting, has been matched in color to the marble in the adjoining bathroom.*

ABOVE: *In the drawing room, John Stefanidis had the oak paneling that dates from 1910 painted white. The fireplace, set in the corner, is adorned with carvings in the manner of Grinling Gibbons. The 18th-century painting depicts the Irish Hell Fire Club.*

RIGHT: *The window seat is covered in striped chintz, and Italian 17th-century chairs provide seating around a Queen Anne table.*

INTERIOR DECOR THAT RESPECTS GRAND SPACES

According to John Stefanidis, the well-known London-based interior designer, the 17th-century house represented "the kind of architecture that has to be respected." And the suite of rooms, which included a sitting room, a drawing room, a dining room, and a bedroom, demanded what Stefanidis called "a conventional treatment."

That meant making very few structural alterations and furnishing the large sedate spaces with the "correct cultural references." Nevertheless, Stefanidis has managed to imbue the rather grand rooms with a special kind of charm—mixing modern drawings with antique paintings, having the walls painted or stenciled in pale colors, and using his own fabric designs for the window treatments and upholstery.

"Because my design philosophy has to do with the necessity and use of space, I believe that decoration is always an addition," Stefanidis explained.

ABOVE: *On a table in the sitting room that is covered with a Bokhara embroidery, two lamps designed by Stefanidis flank a Matisse drawing.*

LEFT: *A large 18th-century Irish secretary stands in the sitting room, which is adjacent to the bedroom. The walls have been stenciled to look like faded old silk.*

LEFT: *An open folio on Palladio is displayed on an architect's table between two windows in the living room. The window treatment, chintz curtains and roll-up blinds, is intentionally fussy and grand.*

ABOVE: *Real candles are lit in the 18th-century porcelain chandelier. The set of calligraphic drawings on the wall is by Millington Drake, a contemporary English artist. Full-height doors allow the room to be closed off from the adjoining drawing room.*

ABOVE RIGHT AND RIGHT: *In the bedroom, roller blinds cover the windows. The bed dates from the late 18th century and the chaise longue is from the Regency period. A 17th-century Persian rug is on the floor.*

LEFT: *The walls have been sponged with paint. An eclectic assortment of personal objects is arranged on the bookshelves.*

RIGHT: *The living room is a mix of junk-shop finds and furniture designed by Hooper. The coffee table was based on an 1810 Regency design by Thomas Hope. The white cotton fabric hides a storage area.*

BELOW: *A vase of dead roses has been deliberately left standing on a wall-hung plaster console.*

ARTFUL WAYS FOR TENEMENT

Although it was located in what Philip Hooper, a young interior designer, described as "a rather seedy area near King's Cross," the two-bedroom flat in a 50-year-old tenement building gave Hooper his first opportunity to decorate a place for himself. "I started with nothing," Hooper said, "and things sort of came together as I went along." The flat achieves a sense of style not only with flair but also with very simple means.

The furniture is of his own design or various junk-shop finds; the stippled walls and marbleized doors—also the designer's handiwork—as well as the dried roses contribute to the flat's surreal effect. "They started out alive," Hooper explained. "When they died, I just kept them. I like slightly sinister things."

ABOVE: *A piece of cashmere crewel-work hangs on a rail above the doorway between the living room and bedroom.*

LEFT: *The sofa and easy chairs have loose cushions covered in bits of fabric that the designer found in antiques shops. A number of architectural etchings are displayed on the wall.*

LEFT: *A bookcase holds a collection of 1930s and 1940s ceramics by the English designer Susie Cooper. Ivory and mother-of-pearl boxes are centered on a length of Victorian damask on the coffee table.*

ABOVE: *In the bedroom, pale yellow cotton fabric has been pleated and stapled to wood battens on the walls. A portrait of the designer is by the foot of the bed.*

RIGHT: *The bedcover has been made from fabric silk-screened by Ann Collins in a yellow, black, and ivory pattern. Cotton has also been used for the voluminous window curtains.*

ABOVE: *The exterior of the Victorian building on the Thames contrasts with the high-tech interior of the flat.*

RIGHT: *Paul Grunfeld took down all the interior walls and with Jake Morton, a designer, completely restructured the apartment, installing a high-tech framework of joists and pillars.*

VICTORIAN FAÇADE, HIGH-TECH CORE

Few interiors provide a more surprising contrast to their exterior than the one belonging to Paul Grunfeld, a young design student who occupies what was once a five-room flat in a building south of the River Thames in London. "I wanted to be able to have a continuous look at the river," explained Grunfeld, who took down all the interior walls and created a miniloft in a Victorian apartment building. The space also illustrates some of his rather unorthodox thoughts on design.

There are traditional Victorian-style moldings on some of the cupboards, while other surfaces are covered with pegboard; there is a storage/bathroom unit that has the sleek look of Italian design of the 1960s, and a bathtub left out in the open; a high-tech garland of electrical wires winds through a metal strut system, and the kitchen and bathroom sink are supported by I-beams.

130

FAR LEFT AND LEFT: *The services have been installed in the center of the apartment. In the open kitchen area, two sinks, both supported by I-beams, are placed side by side, one facing into the kitchen, the other toward the bathroom.*

BELOW FAR LEFT: *A view of the Thames can be appreciated from the bed and from the unenclosed bathtub while bathing.*

BELOW LEFT: *The sleek toilet and storage cubicle has its own ventilation system.*

RIGHT: *The bed has been placed under a bookcase flanked by two cupboards, one finished with traditional Victorian molding, the other made of pegboard, as if it had been remade in the 1950s. The bathtub links the kitchen and sleeping areas.*

STAGE SET FOR A MINIMALIST

"Of course I'd like to have five rooms," admitted John Pawson. The London architecture student lives in a single large room, 680 square feet, in a Victorian terrace house in London's South Kensington. But living in one room is not what makes the apartment particularly unusual.

What distinguishes the space is Pawson's special kind of minimalism. Most of the time it is furnished with only a Le Corbusier table and chairs. "I see the room as a stage set," he explained. "I introduce one object at a time and it is that object that tells you what the room is doing."

So if the space is to be used as a dining room, the table is the dining table; when it becomes an office, a drawing board is brought out of a closet; and when Pawson goes to sleep, he produces a Japanese futon mattress from a cupboard. "Living this way is a compromise. It makes every function into a kind of ritual and requires a lot of discipline. But it's worth it to have the emptiness," he said.

ABOVE: *In the evening, the Le Corbusier table, which is used as a conference table and desk during the day, becomes the dining table. Small candles, set in front of the ornate Victorian fireplace, contribute to the more intimate mood of the room.*

RIGHT: *A large table and side chairs are the only pieces of furniture in the main living space.*

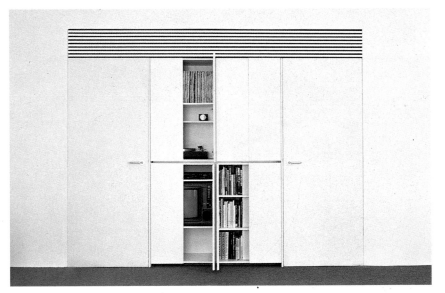

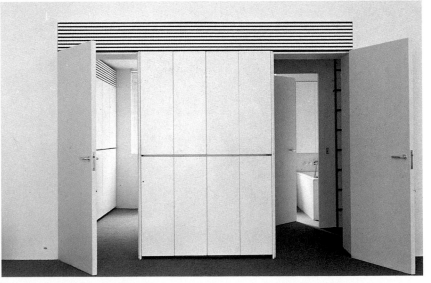

FAR LEFT: *In the tiny hall, stairs lead to a mezzanine bedroom.*

BELOW FAR LEFT: *The Scandinavian Vola taps are the kitchen's only adornment.*

BOTTOM FAR LEFT: *The small kitchen, in which no pots, pans, or dishes are displayed, offers a shiny landscape of stainless steel. A narrow slatted Venetian blind completely covers the window.*

LEFT, BELOW LEFT, AND BOTTOM LEFT: *A ceiling-height door and a series of plain, hardware-free white lacquer cabinets open to reveal their contents, including the television set, stereo system, and books.*

RIGHT: *At night, a black cotton Japanese futon mattress, with yellow tassels, is taken out of a closet and unrolled for sleeping.*

137

OUTRÉ GRANDEUR FOR PIED-À-TERRE

David Hicks's is probably the best known of English names in the field of interior design. The daring mixture of antiques with contemporary pieces, the bold and trend-setting use of pattern on pattern, the imaginative juxtaposition of an array of stylish accessories, have kept Hicks in the forefront of international design for decades.

In many ways, his "chambers," as the London pied-à-terre apartment that he occupies during the week is called, encapsulates his style. It is situated in Albany, the building that was converted in 1804 from an original mansion by Sir William Chambers, the architect of Somerset House. The two-room flat, though small, achieves an outré kind of grandeur.

The materials used in the flat are lavish. The draperies are made of a damask of Hicks's own design, and the bed is surrounded by a canopy and curtains of 18th-century silk damask rewoven for the designer 20 years ago.

ABOVE: *Albany is a prestigious 18th-century mansion off London's Piccadilly.*

ABOVE LEFT: *Oval paintings are symmetrically hung on either side of the fireplace.*

LEFT: *The festoon draperies are made from a David Hicks damask design printed in aubergine on scarlet raw linen. The sofa fabric and carpeting are also by Hicks.*

RIGHT: *Above the accessory-laden mantelpiece, an antique painting hangs on a long ribbon.*

LEFT: *A lavishly appointed and draped bed sits in the center of the bedroom. The inside of the bed curtains is made from 18th-century red silk damask; the outside of the fabric is glazed chintz in a matching color.*

ABOVE: *An antique stand-up desk is near the window in the bedroom.*

RIGHT: *The fireplace in the living room can be glimpsed from the bed.*

AN EVOCATION OF SURREALISM

The interior in a graciously proportioned Edwardian home was done very quickly. But that's the way Julian Powell-Tuck, a young London architect, and his wife, Dinah, tend to work. Although once a dining room, the main living space was transformed into a serene and informal living room. The walls were painted an intense green-blue color, a mosaic inlaid wood floor was put down, and a pair of shelving units were custom-made to look like freestanding pieces.

The antique sofa that was bought at an auction was refinished and reupholstered, and stands in contrast to the shapeless white-sheet-covered chairs. Nick Welch and Claire McLean, who specialize in paint finishes, were responsible for the crackled surfaces on the shelving unit and coffee table. But the focus of the room is the empty picture frame on the wall from which cascades a loose white dust sheet—as evocative an image as it is mysterious.

LEFT: *A new oak mosaic parquet floor and custom-made shelving were installed in the graciously proportioned room.*

BELOW LEFT: *A dust sheet is used as a loose slipcover on one of the easy chairs.*

BOTTOM LEFT: *Objects have been deliberately arranged on the crackled surface of the coffee table.*

RIGHT: *The Victorian sofa, bought at auction, was polished and re-upholstered. A dust sheet cascades from the picture frame.*

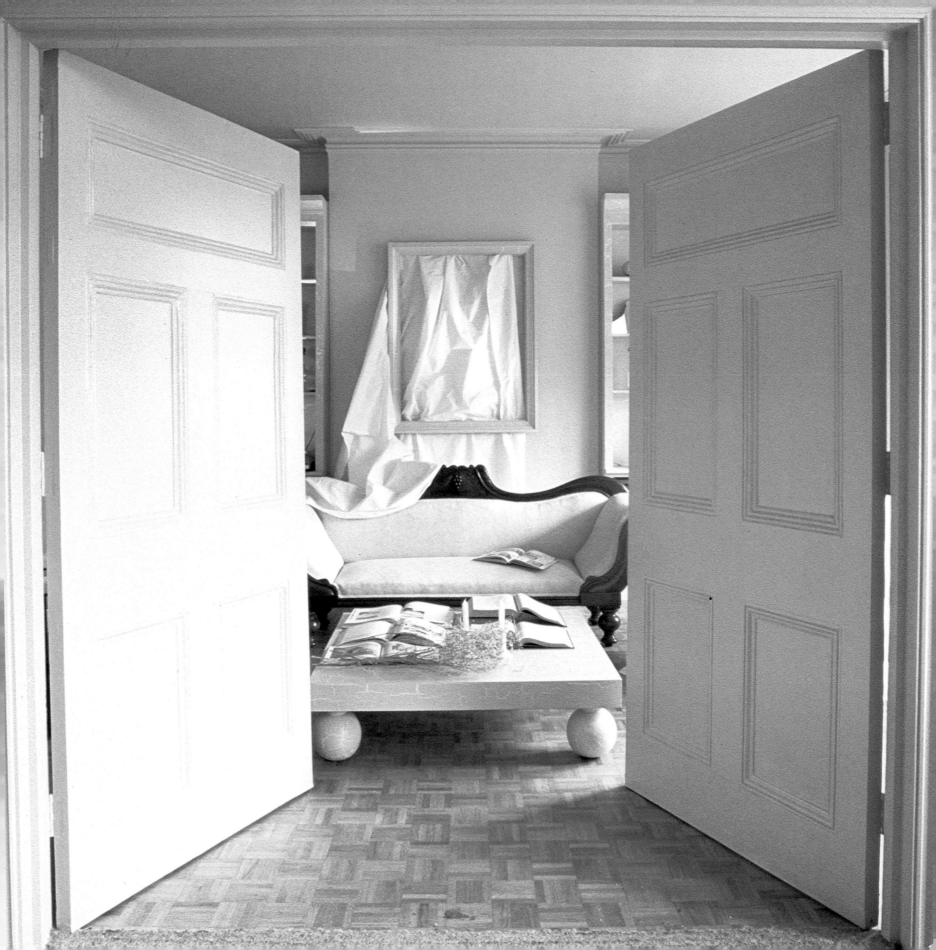

ABOVE: *A vase by Keith Murray, a contemporary potter, is displayed in the shelving unit.*

LEFT, TOP, AND ABOVE: *The pieces of broken mirror, stones, open art books, and red carnations in milk bottles contribute to the surrealistic quality of the interior.*

VERSATILE LAYOUT RECALLS THE 1920s

The building itself, until recently, was not particularly fashionable. Dating from 1932 and boasting its original glass-ceilinged interior vestibule, however, it suited Keith Lichtenstein, a London restaurant owner, admirably.

The flat had a versatile layout and enough wall space to accommodate Lichtenstein's collection of paintings by Gluck, an English portraitist, as well as his 1925 English Poole pottery; Keith Murray's vases from the 1920s; a series of 1902 paintings by Alvaro Guevaro, a South American artist who lived in London; and furniture from the English Arts and Crafts movement. Christopher Baker, an architect who Lichtenstein felt "understood the early 20th-century period," renovated the apartment.

The success of the understated but elegant interior is based on a number of carefully thought-out details. Objects from a given period are modestly

146

grouped together on shelves in half-hidden niches; curtains are only as long as the windows they cover; and the walls throughout the apartment are a subtle off-white color. The frames of the Gluck paintings are painted the same color. "They're meant to always be matched to the walls and to look as if they project from them," said Lichtenstein.

OPPOSITE FAR LEFT: *The exterior of the brick-fronted 1932 apartment building.*

OPPOSITE LEFT AND LEFT: *A glass-ceilinged courtyard serves as a vestibule.*

ABOVE: *The Albert Bridge can be glimpsed from the top-floor balcony.*

LEFT: *Seen from the entrance, the unusual layout of the apartment features a series of rooms that face a wall of windows.*

LEFT: *Hand-painted English Poole pottery, dating from 1925, is displayed on a bookcase between the living room and the bedroom.*

BELOW: *In the kitchen, open shelves hold a collection of pastel-colored vases by Keith Murray.*

BOTTOM: *A 1917 Gluck still life of lilies has been placed over the bathtub. The soft green marble used as its surround was part of a stock of old material.*

RIGHT: *The main focus of the simply furnished bedroom is a series of 1902 sketches of the Marshall Street Baths, a London public bathhouse, by Alvaro Guevaro, a South American painter who lived in England.*

CUSTOM-DESIGNED FOR DRAMA

The Edwardian apartment block off London's Berkeley Square was just the right location for the client, a bachelor who traveled often. But according to Chester Jones, the interior decorator who was commissioned to transform it, "the series of divided and staccato spaces" needed to be opened up to one to another.

The designer's approach involved creating an urbane, dramatic, contemporary look while retaining the building's architectural details. Many of the furniture pieces were designed especially for the apartment by the decorator.

In the striking dining room, the pièces de résistance include an Egyptian daybed and a painting by George Frederic Watts.

ABOVE: *The foyer with its comfortable seating provides extra space for entertaining. A free-standing screen separates the foyer from the living room.*

LEFT: *In the foyer, a pair of 18th-century mother-of-Oriental-pearl lacquer boxes are placed on an altar table that was designed by Chester Jones.*

RIGHT: *In the dining room, a drawing by Egon Schiele is hung over the sideboard, which was also designed by the interior decorator. The two cabochon vases are thought to be Japanese and to date from the 19th century.*

LEFT, BELOW LEFT, AND BOTTOM LEFT: *A pivoting paneled screen separates the dining room from the entrance foyer, allowing the space to be closed off or opened to the rest of the apartment. The interior decorator designed the dining room table to contribute to the Egyptian feeling of the room.*

RIGHT: *An Egyptian daybed, a painting of Mount Ararat by George Frederic Watts, and a bronze panther are set off by dramatic lighting. A small desk has been custom-made to fit into the window recess.*

CONVERSIONS

Although mews houses, the small-scaled structures that were once stables, have long been in demand for residential use, living in buildings that were not originally designed as homes is for the most part a particularly un-English idea. But in the last few years, many commercial warehouses and factories in areas like Covent Garden, originally the site of London's flower garden, and Bermondsey, one of Charles Dickens's preferred haunts, are being converted into residential lofts, inspired by New York's SoHo. There are also quirkier examples. What could be more romantic than settling down in a former gypsy caravan or spending weekends in a Gothic-windowed aviary? Or, as shown here and on the following pages, Clive Evans's solution may be one of the most appealing. His narrow boat combines past traditions and modern efficiency. Although Evans has neither address nor telephone number, he has a freedom to navigate the canals of Britain in a way that many of us can envy.

The custom-built and traditionally decorated long boat that would once have carried cargo is now a private home.

Model of a village hall, with a medieval tower, made in 1880.

CARGO SPACE FOR LIVING

"I found out about long-boats around ten years ago and got absorbed in the whole thing and maybe a bit carried away," admitted Clive Evans, a product designer who now lives on a boat exactly like those that used to carry coal and other merchandise on the English canals.

After searching unsuccessfully for a secondhand boat, Evans decided to have one made from scratch by Malcolm Braine, whose reputation is for "building the Rolls-Royce of narrow boats." And because the boat he ordered—an exact replica of a traditional long-boat—did not have to carry cargo, the designer was able to use the extra space for living.

Evans painted the rose-and-castle decorations that are true in detail to those of an old-fashioned working boat. He also trimmed the small cabin behind the engine room with lace. "The boat families were poor and the decorations were their only real form of affluence and pride," he explained. Known as the boatman's cabin, the diminutive room is now Evans's bedroom.

In what would once have been the cargo area, Evans designed a modern, high-tech, and predominantly black, red, and white living room, studio, and kitchen. Here all is economy and restraint, with such convenient space-saving devices as pull-out work tops and folding furniture.

FAR LEFT AND LEFT: *Clive Evans at the helm of his longboat.*

BELOW FAR LEFT: *The boatman's cabin is situated behind the engine room. The exterior has been decorated with traditional patterns.*

BELOW LEFT AND BOTTOM LEFT: *The narrow boat travels on the Grand Union canal in Central London. Evans had the vessel built from scratch.*

BOTTOM FAR LEFT: *A galvanized-metal container known as a Buckby can was for keeping fresh drinking water.*

RIGHT, FAR RIGHT, BELOW RIGHT, AND BELOW FAR RIGHT: *The designer decorated the boatman's cabin in the traditional way, with paintings of castles and roses, lace trimmings, and ribbon-edged china plates. The bed linens are a modern interpretation of barge roses by Susan Collier. Cooking, heating, eating, and sleeping functions were imaginatively incorporated into a tiny area.*

FAR LEFT AND CENTER FAR LEFT: *In the space that once was meant to carry cargo, Evans installed a living room with a futon sofa that doubles as a guest bed.*

CENTER LEFT: *The tiny but compact bathroom includes a shower and small sink.*

LEFT: *A table is set up on the front end of the boat for alfresco dining.*

BELOW FAR LEFT: *The tiny galley kitchen has been equipped with a number of space-saving devices, including pull-out cutting surfaces, clamp-on lamps, and shallow counter tops.*

LEFT: *The studio and office is Evans's laboratory for researching furniture designs for small spaces.*

RIGHT: *The kitchen is a model of space-saving miniaturization. Narrow shelves hold equipment while small drawers allow for everything to be neatly stored away.*

WORKSHOP IN GEORGIAN WING

Ten years ago, David Mellor, the Yorkshire designer and manufacturer, and his wife, Fiona MacCarthy, the writer, bought Broom Hall to accommodate both their home and Mellor's studio and workshop. Once Sheffield's imposing manor house, the earliest part of the building dates from the late 15th century. There have been alterations over the years, including the cloaking of the original timber-frame building in stone and the addition of a Georgian wing.

"I decided to go back to the 1780 plan," Mellor said, "and to install the workshops in the Georgian wing because it could provide the necessary big open rooms." The rest of the house, with its smaller spaces, was converted into living quarters. The renovation involved restoring the library to the way it was in the late 15th century and building a kitchen that is physically as well as figuratively the center of the household. Throughout, Mellor has favored such natural materials as English elm for the floors, English oak, and quarry tiles.

ABOVE LEFT: *Polishing and grinding machines were installed in the large rooms.*

LEFT: *The design studio has been furnished with Alvar Aalto pieces.*

RIGHT: *The Georgian wing that now houses the cutlery workshop and factory dates from 1780.*

LEFT: *The Georgian east wing is connected to an earlier 16th-century building.*

BELOW LEFT: *A detail of one of the façades of the timber-frame part of the house complex.*

RIGHT: *Furniture by Alvar Aalto has also been used in the renovated library. The timber frame has been taken apart and reassembled. The newly installed wood floors are of English elm.*

164

LEFT: *The spacious kitchen takes up the center part of the house. The floors are of Staffordshire blue quarry tiles and the cabinets were made of natural English oak. In the cooking area, counter tops are of stainless steel. The kitchen table is made of a thick slab of solid beech wood that is supported by a galvanized-steel frame. The chairs are by Ernest Gimson, the well-known craftsman.*

RIGHT: *Stone steps lead from the exterior to the entrance hall and kitchen. The chair is an early black oak Gimson design.*

RIGHT AND BELOW RIGHT: *The spacious master bedroom is sparsely furnished. Pictures are lined up on the wall behind a Gimson chair; an ornate Victorian sofa is displayed like a piece of sculpture.*

PRIVACY IN AN OPEN PLAN

Once a hat factory and warehouse, and dating from 1879, the building in the vicinity of St. Paul's Cathedral was converted a few years ago into open-plan residential lofts. The two 2,000-square-foot top floors were made into a three-bedroom apartment and a painting studio.

All the walls were replastered, a new maple floor was installed, and the interior space was organized to allow for some open areas as well as a number of separate, private areas. Piers Gough, a London-based architect, worked on the renovation project.

The loft was meticulously thought out, from the generously proportioned sitting area to the book-lined work space. One of the main problems was how to put a lot of disparate furniture together in the same general space, because in a more conventional type of house the pieces would have been in different rooms. Solutions included using the larger pieces, such as an old Welsh pine dresser, low stepped walls, and long bookcases as room dividers.

RIGHT: *Ornate late-19th-century* ·*cast-iron columns punctuate the 2,000-square-foot loft.*

RIGHT: *The entrance, flanked by stepped storage units and two radiators, is a double door set into a curved wall.*

BELOW: *The factory building's original staircase links the main living space to the artist's studio on the floor above.*

RIGHT: *Two sofas by Eileen Gray and a chair by Charles Eames provide comfortable seating. The gas-and-coal fireplace is the focus of the living area.*

LEFT: *The master bedroom has an antique French box bed with a headboard that looks like a huge picture frame.*

BELOW: *A collection of artworks is carefully lined up along the wall. An Art Deco lamp stands on a small side table.*

LEFT: *Matching American wedding-ring quilts cover the Art Deco twin beds in one of the bedrooms.*

FAR LEFT AND LEFT: *The Art Deco figurines and a circular Art Deco cabinet are some of the furnishings that needed to be integrated in the loft space.*

BELOW FAR LEFT AND BELOW LEFT: *A long curved wall, filled with books, spans the loft and provides an area for the study.*

BOTTOM FAR LEFT: *A Welsh cabinet facing the kitchen is used to store and display china. It also acts as a partition for the dining area.*

BOTTOM LEFT: *An inscription marks the antique chair in the dining area as having once belonged to the 18th-century English artist William Hogarth.*

RIGHT: *The metal spiral stairway with wood treads that connects the two floors of the loft was custom-made so as to be wide enough for two people to pass.*

173

FAMILY HOME IN METHODIST CHAPEL

In 1968, a late-19th-century Methodist chapel in Wiltshire was converted by William Gough Howell, an architect, into a country house for his family. The building had included two large rooms, one a chapel, the other a schoolroom.

None of the original chapel fittings was wasted: the pulpit was transformed into a bedroom, the communion rail was turned into a sofa frame, and the wood boards from the pews were made into tabletops, floorboards, and kitchen cabinetry. The cast-iron columns came from a demolished building.

ABOVE: *The chapel was converted into a country house 15 years ago.*

ABOVE LEFT: *The 100-year-old quilt was made by a group of women who attended the chapel and were members of a temperance league.*

LEFT: *The entrance to the kitchen area is enclosed below the pulpit.*

RIGHT: *The main space includes a living area, a dining area, and a full-size pool table.*

AN AMERICAN-INFLUENCED TANNERY LOFT

Michael Baumgarten, an American architectural designer who moved to England in the early 1970s, admits that his approach to the mid-19th-century building was very much influenced by the conversion of lofts in New York's SoHo area.

Situated in Bermondsey, within view of London's famous Tower Bridge, the brick, cast-iron, and timber-truss structure dates from 1864 and was originally a tannery. Reflecting the more advanced doctrines of the late 19th century, its interior spaces are not dark and claustrophobic but light-filled and airy. "It was basically a typical Victorian warehouse," explained Baumgarten, who created six co-ops in the building, as well as the 3,000-square-foot expanse in which he both lives and works.

Central heating and fireproofing were installed, plumbing lines brought up to each floor, and maple strip flooring laid.

In his own space, Baumgarten insulated the ceiling with foil-backed fiberglass. Because he wanted to keep the main living area uncluttered and open, he designed what he called the Blue Tower, which houses the kitchen, bathroom, and bedroom in the middle of the loft.

FAR LEFT ABOVE AND ABOVE: *A mid-19th-century tannery was converted into residential lofts by Michael Baumgarten, an American architectural designer.*

FAR LEFT: *From the loft's arched windows, a view of Tower Bridge can be glimpsed.*

LEFT: *The Blue Tower, a structure that encompasses the loft's kitchen, bedroom, and bathroom, is at the center of the space.*

RIGHT AND FAR RIGHT: *Stepped cupboards provide storage space under the tower stairs.*

BELOW: *The renovation included the installation of central heating. Radiators are set into a continuous shelf under the large windows.*

RIGHT: *The living area has been left open and is furnished with a large sofa, Lloyd Loom chairs, and O.M.K. metal mesh-frame chairs by Rodney Kinsman.*

BELOW: *A long wooden drain-board and circular sinks are part of the custom-designed kitchen.*

LEFT: *Part of the kitchen counter extends from the tower behind the stairs. A square dining table seats eight people.*

CARAVAN WITH SCENIC PAST

Although for the past six years it has been the home of John Pockett, the caravan, built in 1915 for £850, has had quite a varied existence. The British film director Peter Rogers once used it as a retreat and an elderly nurse who took care of gypsy children traveled around in it. The original owner, a Tilly Winters, ran swing boat rides and coconut shies at fairgrounds.

On the inside, panels have been painted with scenes from the 1925 epic film *Ben Hur,* and the etched window in the roof is ruby-colored glass. Pockett, who is now restoring the caravan to its former glory, also decorates and restores caravans for others in Cookham, a small town in Berkshire.

LEFT: *Panels of etched glass are set into the door. The handle has been cut from a piece of amber glass.*

BELOW LEFT: *Feathers, traditionally associated with the Prince of Wales, adorn the door and were meant to give a royal touch to the caravan's livery.*

RIGHT: *The exterior of the gypsy caravan is highly decorated. Steps are pulled down when the structure is not in motion. Most of the cooking would have been done on a stove outdoors.*

LEFT: *A pair of doors below the bed open to provide sleeping accommodations for children. Etched mirrors slide closed and panels of ruby-colored glass have been set into the ceiling.*

RIGHT: *Paintings depicting the movie* Ben Hur *were used to decorate the interior.*

FAR RIGHT: *An old-fashioned paraffin lamp was a source of atmospheric as well as ambiant light.*

BELOW RIGHT: *A collection of Crown Derby and Royal Worcester china fills the cabinet, and was displayed as a sign of prosperity.*

BELOW FAR RIGHT: *A coal stove with a small oven was used for warmth and some cooking.*

NESTING IN AN OLD AVIARY

Situated on the Audley End estate in Essex, the small building, dating from 1776, was modeled after designs by the architect Robert Adam for a chapel on the estate, and was used as an aviary.

Elizabeth Hanley, who is known for her handmade lamps and lampshades, happened upon the house when she visited friends nearby. "It was like a folly in the woods," she recalled. "The building was completely derelict and had a tree growing out of the roof. But I fell in love with it."

The original 18th-century windows and porticos were still intact in the room that had once served as an aviary for rare birds, but the space had a mud floor. Hanley embarked on a major renovation project.

Now, although quite elegant in feeling, the interior has been treated with moderation. "I try to remember that this is still a cottage," Hanley said. "I don't want it to be too grand."

ABOVE LEFT: *The house is nestled among trees.*

LEFT: *In the hall that now doubles as a dining room, there is an 18th-century painting of the Audley End estate.*

TOP AND ABOVE: *The small-scaled building features arched doors and gabled windows that open out onto the garden.*

RIGHT: *The elaborate painted woodwork contributes to the romantic look of the house.*

LEFT: *The renovation of the aviary included making the space that originally housed rare birds into the main sitting room of the house. The furniture is generally small in scale, in keeping with the size of the rooms.*

BELOW LEFT: *A collection of needlepoint pictures of dogs and cats covers a wall in a guest bedroom.*

RIGHT: *Doors and windows frame a number of views of the garden. A stable door opens onto the lawn.*

CENTER RIGHT: *A gazebo in the garden can be glimpsed through one of the arched windows.*

FAR RIGHT: *An antique birdcage that recalls the original use of the house is set on the windowsill.*

RIGHT, CENTER RIGHT, FAR RIGHT: *Three views of the hallway, where a Victorian sculpture is displayed on a painted cupboard.*

ARCHITECT'S TOY FACTORY

Piers Gough came upon the brick structure that stood behind a London house by chance. Built by the suffragettes as a toy factory in World War I, it had had, according to the architect, "a checkered career." He bought it in 1975.

Because the factory consisted only of two rooms, one above the other, Gough extended the building with a turretlike space that includes a staircase, guest room, and bathroom. Plumbing and central heating were also installed. The top floor featured a pitched roof which the architect felt was most suitable for the main living area. The kitchen, with its marbleized sink unit, has been situated at one end of the spacious room. Most of the furnishings in the house were collected over the years from flea markets or were acquired when Derry & Toms and Biba, two London department stores, closed.

BELOW: *The brick building, converted into a residence, is now surrounded by a garden.*

In the living room, the mottled ceiling and damp patches on the walls were left untouched. "I wanted a rough-and-ready and quite matter-of-fact look," the architect said.

By contrast, the master bedroom is intentionally soft and luxurious. "Delightfully over-rich," said Gough of the pink-carpeted room that boasts a rare cast-iron sink and bathtub that are displayed like free-standing sculpture.

FAR LEFT: *The pitched roof made the top floor the most suitable as the main living area.*

BELOW FAR LEFT: *The furniture includes a pair of hairdresser's chairs and two 1940s armchairs.*

LEFT: *Off-white, heavy cotton sheeting has been used for the curtains. The top of the unstitched material has been clamped between two poles.*

BELOW: *A red metal handrail adorns the plywood spiral staircase, which has been built inside the new turretlike extension.*

ABOVE: *Large stockpots and other kitchen equipment are conveniently hung from hooks in the ceiling.*

LEFT: *Two lamps as well as a colorful collection of china, mostly from Portugal, are set out on what was once a cake stand from the Biba department store.*

RIGHT: *In the kitchen area, the sink unit, painted in marble trompe l'oeil by Paul and Janet Czainski, has an altarlike quality. The Roman-numeral equivalent of 1978 marks the year of its completion. Above the sink, dishes drip dry on a pair of wall-hung racks.*

ABOVE: *In the pink-hued master bedroom, a rare cast-iron sink and bathtub have been installed out in the open.*

RIGHT: *The mirrors that flank the door originally came from the Biba department store.*

FAR RIGHT: *The metal curtain rods are twisted at either end.*

RIGHT: *The bedroom suite is from the 1950s. The cast-iron radiators project into the room like screens. A satin belt by the Japanese fashion designer Kansai Yamamoto snakes up the lamp.*

BELOW: *A row of light fixtures is hung in the downstairs hallway. Clothes are stored on a 30-foot-long rail or in a display unit.*

BOTTOM: *Diamond-shaped tiles of mirror top the dressing table.*

COUNTRY HOUSES

The English countryside has always held a magical appeal to Britishers and foreigners alike. Being in the country, as a full-time resident or weekend visitor, seems to be a vital requirement for English living. Nestled in beautifully landscaped parks, the grand stately homes represent the enduring tradition of English country life. But the same can be said for the more modest stone or thatch houses that are their owners' pride and joy. Fixing up a ramshackle cottage or working in the garden are not usually considered chores. Rather, Britishers derive a great deal of pleasure from embellishing their country retreats. Sometimes the furnishings are matched to the house's exterior, but often the choice of contemporary pieces contrasts dramatically with the rustic charm of the house.

The row of stone houses is a typical Cotswolds village scene.

English stately home interpreted in an 1880 dollhouse.

LETTING LIGHT INTO STONE HOUSE

A country house rarely requires as much of a renovation as the one undertaken by an artist in the Cotswolds. When the 200-year-old stone house was purchased 12 years ago, it was in disrepair. And because the interior was dark, an entire section of the second floor was removed so as to let light from what were once the upstairs windows into the ground floor.

Although the original roof of the cottage was made of thatch, it had been recovered in stone. And the interesting configurations of the ceilings in the second floor bedrooms are the result of the thatch being weighed down by the stone over the years.

ABOVE: *In the low-ceilinged living room, the wood beams have been painted green.*

RIGHT: *The niche in the wall was once a fireplace in an upstairs bedroom. The small window above the front door lets light into the entrance hall.*

RIGHT: *Art Deco figurines and Wedgwood plates decorate the fireplace.*

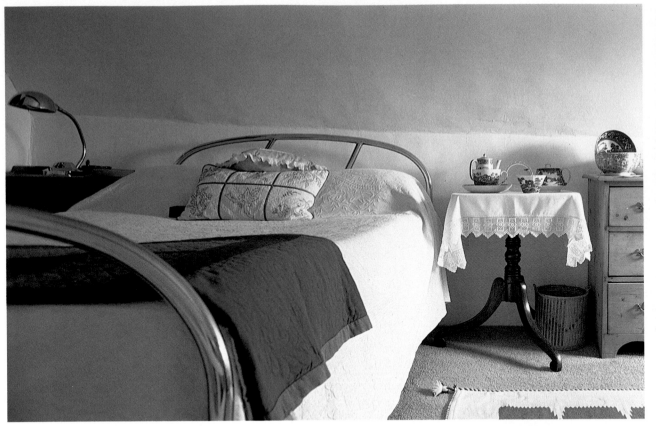

ABOVE: *In one of the guest bedrooms, an American Amish quilt is folded on a 1930s tubular steel bed. A delicate white lace-trimmed cloth covers the bedside table.*

RIGHT: *A row of pitchers is lined up behind the bed.*

FAR RIGHT: *The headboard in the master bedroom is part of an antique French bedroom suite. The blanket that is used as a bedcover was woven by an itinerant American craftsman.*

TOP: *A large wardrobe dominates the master bedroom. Navajo rugs are draped over the sofa.*

ABOVE: *The window is set into a recess in the stone wall.*

A VENETIAN VILLA ON A BUCOLIC SITE

It was known as the Temple of the Four Seasons, possibly because the plaster reliefs in the rooms depicted the different times of the year. The mid-18th-century country house, thought to be by Sir Robert Taylor, was built as a prototype for the architect's Palladian-style villas. Charles Beresford-Clark, a London antiques dealer, spent over three and a half years on the renovation of the pavilion, relying more on design ingenuity than on money.

"The feeling is that of a Venetian house set down in the English countryside," said Clark. The ornamental canal was built at the same time as the villa, and Beresford-Clark frequently convinces weekend guests that they should help dig and restore the waterway before sitting down to their Sunday lunch.

ABOVE LEFT AND RIGHT: *The Palladian-style villa dates from 1760, and the canal is now filled with carp.*

LEFT: *The dining room with its oval window that overlooks the canal is furnished with an antique oil lamp and contemporary French chestnut chairs.*

BELOW: *A tea cozy made by a friend depicts the villa.*

ABOVE: *The staircase, original to the house, had to be completely restored.*

ABOVE RIGHT AND RIGHT: *What was once the villa's "saloon," a room used in the 18th century for summer suppers, has been converted into the main living area. The chandelier is Italian and dates from the 18th century. Informal cotton slipcovers contrast with the yellow-walled room's grandeur.*

ABOVE: *A small staircase leads to a sleeping area over the dressing room.*

LEFT: *Because Beresford-Clark thought a sofa would not be appropriate for the "saloon," he had a freestanding banquette made and covered it in French mattress ticking.*

REDESIGN FOR OLD MANOR

The sprawling house in Great Linford, Buckinghamshire, has had a complex history. Parts of the structure date from the 12th century, others from Edwardian times, but the main building is Elizabethan. Once used as a hospital as well as a rectory, the building was bought in 1976 by Derek Walker, an architect and town planner.

Walker undertook the renovation of what he described as a "building and outbuildings, all in a very bad state," and created private living quarters for himself as well as an office for 30 people. Because of the size of the complex—12,500 square feet—the renovation was a major project. And while Walker retained many of the house's older architectural detailing, he decided to furnish the rooms with modern pieces—including designs by Mies van der Rohe and Charles Eames.

TOP LEFT: *The main part of the sprawling house dates from the early 16th century.*

ABOVE LEFT: *The entrance hall has a Victorian floor and an Elizabethan staircase.*

LEFT AND RIGHT: *The living room has been furnished with classic modern pieces as well as some custom-made sofas designed by the architect. The fireplace is a recent addition and acts as a focus in the large room.*

STONE HOUSE REDONE WITH RURAL CHARM

The late-18th-century house was in basically good condition when it was bought about four years ago by Lesley Astaire, a London interior decorator, and her husband, Bill Jacklin, the painter. Nevertheless, the gray stone house that is situated in the Oxfordshire Cotswolds had to be completely repainted.

"It took us two weeks to paint, decorate, and move in," Astaire explained. "I like things to look lived in immediately. Good furniture and lighting are most important to me. The house was large enough for a number of separate areas—living room, an informal breakfast area, and a more formal space for dining.

The rooms were furnished with objects from the couple's two previous homes, including a 19th-century Japanese settee, some kilim rugs, a 1920s mirror, American blue-and-white spatterware, and a collection of 18th-century Leeds china. "As time has gone by," she said, "I've become less disciplined in what I put together."

LEFT: *The gray stone house was built about 1780.*

FAR LEFT: *In the hallway near the front door, a plush tablecloth has been hung on a rod to shield the interior from drafts. A 19th-century French mirror has been hung over a 19th-century carved Japanese settee.*

BELOW LEFT: *In the kitchen, baskets and cooking equipment are suspended from a ceiling rack. The miniature stove was once a Victorian salesman's sample.*

RIGHT: *Wicker and chestnut chairs surround a table in the informal breakfast area. The watercolor on the wall was a junk-shop find. A collection of American blue-and-white spatterware fills the shelving unit.*

ABOVE: *The master bedroom has antique American quilts, French hand-printed cotton curtains, and a set of French 1920s enamel brushes on the dressing table.*

FAR LEFT: *The large living room, a recent addition to the house, was not altered by the current owners. The floor is covered with sisal and the sofas are upholstered in linen and mattress ticking.*

ABOVE LEFT: *Drawings by Allen Jones and David Tindle as well as some pieces of 18th-century Leeds china are lined up on the shelves in the living room.*

LEFT: *A Chinese lamp stands on an early 19th-century English tree table. The linoleum prints are by the 1930s artist Claude Flight.*

MODERN DESIGNS IN QUEEN ANNE HOUSE

Some of the yew trees were there even before the country house was built in 1728. The elegant Queen Anne building, situated on the edge of the Savernake Forest in Wiltshire, included a latter Victorian wing. "We wanted to bring the main house back to the way it was in the early 18th century," said Brian Henderson, a London-based architect who lives there with his wife, Elizabeth. It took the couple a number of years of major renovation work before they could move in.

The interior is particularly striking because the Hendersons chose to furnish the period house with exclusively contemporary pieces, including designs by Vico Magistretti and Alvar Aalto. "I live in the 20th century," Henderson explained, "and I am an architect who feels that it is important to make a statement about one's own time."

OPPOSITE ABOVE FAR LEFT AND FAR LEFT: *The house with its early Victorian addition is surrounded by yew, beech, and chestnut trees. The garden bench is a reproduction of an Edwin Lutyens design.*

OPPOSITE BELOW FAR LEFT: *Dusty Miller, the gardener, on the property.*

LEFT AND ABOVE: *The checked stone floor dates from the early 18th century. The stones that are used as doorstops came from an island in the Scottish Hebrides.*

TOP: *The ornamental staircase that opens onto a spacious landing is original to the house.*

ABOVE: *An etching by Richard Hamilton hangs on the wall behind a black lacquer table. The lamp is Italian.*

LEFT: *The bookcases in the work-room are by Vico Magistretti, an Italian designer.*

LEFT: *In the Victorian wing, a plant-filled room opens onto the garden. The floors are covered with brown quarry tiles.*

BELOW: *Personal memorabilia and a collection of graphic works cover a wall in the library.*

ABOVE: *A small library outside the bedroom has floor-to-ceiling book-shelves by Alvar Aalto.*

RIGHT: *Brian and Elizabeth Henderson designed the velvet-covered bed in the master bedroom.*

BELOW RIGHT: *The bathroom has white marble walls, a cork floor, and brass fixtures that are reproductions of old hardware.*

BELOW: *A closet with brass rods for shoes links the bathroom to the master bedroom.*

RIGHT: *The typical farmhouse dresser was in the kitchen of the house long before its recent renovation. It is now filled with blue-and-white chinaware.*

BELOW RIGHT: *Pots and pans and cooking equipment are stored on a wire rack above a butcher-block worktable by the stove.*

BOTTOM RIGHT: *Herbs are hung to dry in the stone larder that has existed since Victorian times.*

RIGHT: *Clear glasses, a coffeepot, and white French stacking china have been grouped on bull-nosed shelves in the kitchen, which is in the early Victorian wing.*

UPDATED ROOMS FOR A WORKING FARM

Situated in Norfolk, the house is still part of a working farm that grows sugar beets, wheat, and potatoes. The oldest part of the building dates from the 17th century, and David Bennett's father and grandfather both lived there at one time.

But while the exterior is the same white-painted brick that existed in the previous generation, Bennett, with the help of London designer and antiques dealer Piers von Westenholz, has completely transformed the interior. The rooms, traditional in decor, have been updated with unusual colors. Bennett has incorporated classical antiques, custom-made pieces, and objects collected on travels abroad.

ABOVE AND ABOVE RIGHT: *The exterior of the farmhouse is of painted brick. The topiary forms are meant to support rosebushes.*

RIGHT: *The hound statue came from Normandy and now stands on a Regency butler's bed chest in the hall.*

ABOVE: *The chicken wire that covers the fronts of the bookcases in the living room has been painted in a crisscross design.*

ABOVE LEFT: *In the living room the comfortable seating has been upholstered in a Colefax & Fowler chintz.*

LEFT: *The bookcases were especially designed for the living room.*

LEFT: *The original beams in the dining room were repainted in bright blue. The table is covered with a coordinated blue-and-white checked cloth.*

ABOVE AND BELOW: *The stencil work on the floor in the dining room was done by Mary McCarthy and based on a wheat motif to represent one of the working farm's main crops.*

ABOVE: *The fireplace in the study is surrounded by a brass guard.*

RIGHT: *The study has been boldly decorated in red and green. Canvas shades cover the windows.*

BELOW: *A kilim rug has been used as the upholstery on the sofa.*

TOP: *The master bedroom is simply furnished. Two small mahogany tables have been placed near a Regency bed.*

ABOVE AND RIGHT: *The upstairs landing has been painted all in white. Black-and-white engravings are hung in the stairway.*

ABOVE: *Although completely renovated, a claw-footed bathtub was retained in the bathroom.*

LEFT: *In another bathroom, the tiles behind the bathtub have been painted in trompe l'oeil stencil by Mary McCarthy.*

ABOVE LEFT: *The main guest room features a half-tester bed that was found in Norfolk.*

LEFT: *The walls are covered in fabric. An antique quilt has been draped over the table.*

OLD HOUSE, INFORMAL MIX

For the last four and a half years Rupert and Sally Watts and their two children have lived in the middle of farmlands near Cambridge.

The house was built in 1632, the date carved over the huge walk-in fireplace where logs are burned all winter, and when the couple bought the thatch-roof house, it had been used as dog kennels and was very run down. The couple undertook most of the renovation work on their own and furnished the interior with an informal combination of old and new pieces, a point of view characterized by a mix of country charm and modern classic designs.

ABOVE: *The 17th-century thatch-roof farmhouse is set on a hill amid farmlands.*

LEFT: *All the beams, doors, and brickwork in the house were stripped by sandblasting.*

ABOVE: *The living room is furnished with a country-style coffee table, side table, and chest, as well as with a comfortable sofa upholstered in a fabric by Susan Collier. The walls have been sponged to create a stippled effect.*

ABOVE: *In the dining area, classic Bauhaus chairs are placed around a long wood refectory table that was once in Rupert Watts's nursery. The lathe and plaster between the beams has been replaced with glass, to give a view into the plant-filled conservatory.*

LEFT: *Some of the wooden beams pre-date the farmhouse and are thought to have been taken from an earlier structure.*

ABOVE: *The master bedroom has been installed in the attic where the chickens used to live.*

LEFT: *The old doors have traditional wooden latches.*

ABOVE: *The garden of the Elizabethan house boasts a beech-wood arch and clipped box hedges.*

RIGHT AND BELOW RIGHT: *The red brick house, which is surrounded by a moat, was built as a hunting lodge in the second half of the 16th century.*

A DECORATOR'S HUNT LODGE

David Mlinaric thinks that his family's country house was built in the second half of the 16th century by a man who used it as a hunting lodge and would periodically move his whole entourage there for months at a time. But when the London-based interior decorator took over the Elizabethan house, which is surrounded on all sides by a fish-filled moat, he simplified the layout of the rooms that had been divided by the previous owner by taking down a number of walls.

"In the summer we live in the garden, in the winter in the sitting room, a family room—with its fireplace, gramophones, television, and children running all around," Mlinaric explained. Although the house is spacious on the whole, the interior is not overwhelmingly grand.

Rather, the decorator has adopted a fairly understated and traditional approach. The walls are all painted the same light color; the furnishings, mostly English and French country antiques, have been collected over the years.

The dining room is dominated by an unusual wood and plaster sculptural piece that has been hung over the fireplace. "I've no idea what it is," Mlinaric admitted. "I bought it a while ago from a junk shop in Battersea. I'm always looking forward to finding out more about it one day."

LEFT: *In the entrance, coats and summer hats are hung on stags' antlers that wind up the wall. Pairs of rubber boots are kept in a neat line underneath.*

ABOVE: *Guests who spend the night are asked to sign the visitor's book, which is kept on a table in the hall.*

LEFT: *In the dining room, the Victorian tree light chandelier over the antique table is lit with candles.*

LEFT: *The large kitchen has uneven brick floors, a pine dresser, and a pine table.*

BELOW: *The unidentified wood and plaster sculpture over the fireplace in the dining room was found in a junk shop.*

ABOVE: *A flower-painted screen has been placed near the door in one of the bedrooms.*

RIGHT: *The bench at the foot of the bed in the oak-beamed guest bedroom is an original piece of outdoor furniture, copies of which are now being reproduced by Chatsworth Carpenters.*

RIGHT: *The master bedroom is dominated by the canopy bed.*

BELOW: *The bathroom sink has been sculpted out of wood.*

LEFT: *Flower trugs are piled under a side table that is flanked by two antique chairs.*

BELOW LEFT: *Two lamps with shades made from ordinance survey maps stand on the 18th-century table in the sitting room.*

RIGHT: *The sitting room, where the family gathers in the winter or on summer evenings, has been comfortably furnished.*

SMALLER HOME NEAR POTTERY FOR DESIGNER

When her husband died a few years ago, Susie Cooper decided to move from the parsonage in which they had lived for 42 years and renovated what had been an outbuilding on the property into a house for herself and her son. "I didn't want to leave the village, and the house had gotten too big," explained the industrial designer, who is well known for her work in china and pottery. "But I wanted to move before I was too decrepit."

ABOVE: *Once an outbuilding on the property, the house was renovated by Susie Cooper, who moved there from the adjoining rectory.*

TOP RIGHT: *Bowls and platters by Cooper are displayed on the windowsill of the bay window.*

ABOVE RIGHT: *The designer's signature marks some of her early pieces of pottery.*

RIGHT: *A corner cupboard in the bedroom features an unfinished Cooper design.*

FAR RIGHT: *The ink-stain-on-wood paintings on the landing are part of a series that Cooper started making in the 1930s.*

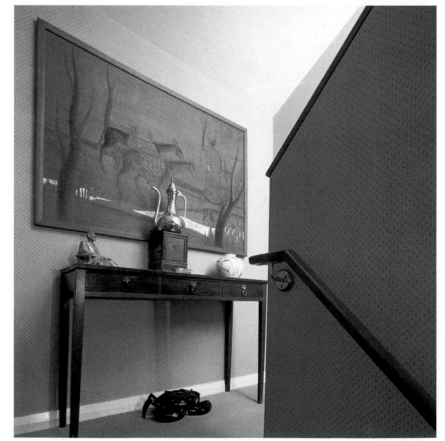

232

Cooper's new home is simply furnished. Some of the possessions she kept when she moved included her ink-stain-on-wood paintings that she first did in the 1930s. "They tend to fade," Cooper explained. "Sometimes I try and bring them back again." There are also the hand-decorated dishes she made for herself in the late 1930s and early 1940s.

The house is situated about 11 miles from the Staffordshire Pottery where Cooper prefers to work, rather than at home. "I need to be in a factory atmosphere," she explained. "I'd never do the things I do if I didn't go to the works. I feel it's nice to keep in touch with the factory."

LEFT: *On the dining room table are Cooper's dinner plates with a white leaf motif on a dark green background; the contrasting salad plates have a swirl pattern.*

FAR LEFT, LEFT AND BELOW LEFT: *Burgundy and white stacking snack trays, a tea set, and the breakfast china are also by Cooper.*

ATTIC VIEWS
FOR OLD HOUSE

"We live in the attic," explains Matyelok Gibbs, who shares a stone house in Gloucestershire, 100 miles from London, with Ursula Jones. Both actresses, the women had asked Max Clendinning to help them with the conversion of the stone house, the main part of which is more than 350 years old.

The designer's response was to make windows in the windowless attic so as to take advantage of the views of the countryside, and add a number of small balconies. The top-floor room now includes a kitchen and living area. A double-height room, originally a lean-to that was added to the house, is filled with plants.

The front door opens onto a large hall and living area in which the furniture has been loosely covered with colorful textiles. "These are things I picked up in India," said Gibbs. "The rest is just any old stuff."

ABOVE FAR LEFT AND ABOVE CENTER LEFT: *In the summer, Matyelok Gibbs and Ursula Jones often eat outdoors. A Thai umbrella opens to shield the wood picnic table.*

FAR LEFT: *A stable door opens onto the entrance hall.*

CENTER LEFT: *The circular window in the stairway was installed during the renovation.*

ABOVE LEFT AND RIGHT: *The tall plant-filled room was originally a lean-to addition.*

LEFT: *The carvings that decorate the fireplace came from a 17th-century Flemish door.*

ABOVE: *Because the ground floor was damp, the kitchen and dining area were installed at the top of the house, in what was once the attic.*

LEFT: *The original poster near the dining table is by Alphonse-Marie Mucha, the Art Nouveau artist.*

RIGHT: *The large room on the ground floor has now been made into the living room. The terracotta walls were inspired by the color discovered when the old walls were stripped. The wall hanging and the shawls that are draped over the armchairs are from India, and the chair on the right is an original Charles Rennie Mackintosh design.*

ARISTOCRATIC FAMILY HOME

Weston Hall, the early 18th-century country mansion in Northamptonshire, is an example of the design eccentricities that are associated with the English aristocracy. Built in 1702 by Sir John Blencow as a Valentine's Day gift to his daughter, Susanna Jennens, the rural house has been passed down through the women in the Sitwell family for many generations.

The interior has evolved over the centuries. The present owner, Sir Sacheverell Sitwell, inherited the house from his aunt in the 1920s. His wife, Lady Sitwell, decorated it using pieces of furniture, some of which had been there since Victorian times.

ABOVE: *The main wing of the Sitwell country mansion was added in 1777.*

ABOVE RIGHT: *The front hall is lined with bells that summoned servants to the different rooms.*

RIGHT: *The gilt mirrors belonged to Sir Sacheverell's sister, Dame Edith Sitwell, the writer, who died in 1964.*

ABOVE: *Lady Sitwell commissioned a local craftsman to make the octagonal closet after she had seen one abroad.*

LEFT: *The imposing canopied bed has been in the house since the early 1840s.*

LEFT: *A portrait of Sir Sacheverell's sister Dame Edith Sitwell, the writer, by Pavel Tchelitchew hangs over the bookcases in the library.*

BELOW: *The bookcase over the mantel holds antique leather-bound volumes, and the bell pull on the left was to call the parlor maid.*

PARTICULAR PASSIONS

From the time that well-to-do Britishers of the 18th and 19th centuries began bringing back souvenirs from their travels, collecting has been a particularly English pastime. And the hallmark of English decorating—the cluttered interior with layer upon layer of objects—is a reflection of this obsession. It is an infatuation that involves a need not only to acquire the object itself but everything that surrounds it as well. Whether a particular period is being re-created or a special kind of object searched out, the English hobby of collecting seems more than anything else to be a way of keeping the past alive in the present.

Household packaging and memo-rabilia fill a bookcase in antiques dealer Stephen Long's London apartment kitchen.

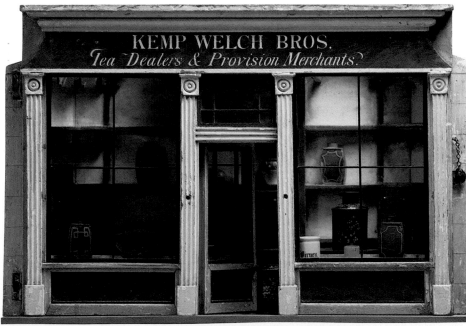

Painted carved wood model of a 19th-century provisions or grocery shop.

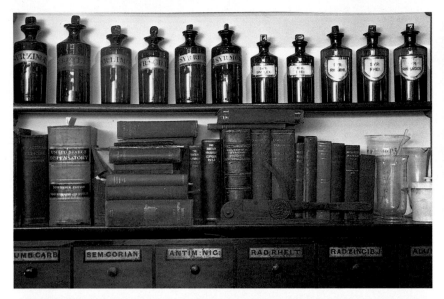

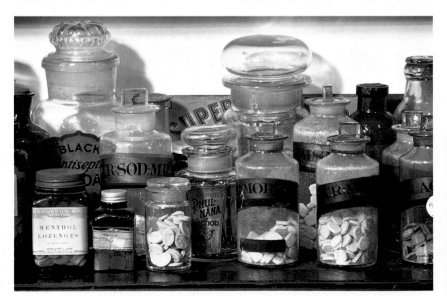

242

PHARMACY PARAPHERNALIA

John Newstead, a pharmacist born near Norwich, returned to his hometown in 1960 to find that many of the old chemist shops he knew from his youth were disappearing. So he started collecting all the chemist-shop paraphernalia and memorabilia that could be acquired. "I accumulated so many things that I had to build something to house it all," he said.

Newstead and his wife, Janie, built a structure in their backyard that is the same size as a typical 1920s chemist shop, and stocked it with authentic bottles filled with medicines, prescription books in Latin, and chemist's apparatus, including pill machines and suppository molds. "Fortunately, when sons took over the business from their fathers, they didn't throw things away but stored them in cellars or attics," said Newstead.

Next year, the Iceni Pharmacy, which Newstead named after a Celtic tribe that roamed England's East Anglia region in ancient times in the same way that he wandered in search of his treasures, will be permanently installed at the Bridewell Museum in Norwich.

LEFT AND RIGHT: *All the fixtures, bottles, and medicines that John and Janie Newstead collected for the chemist's shop are authentic.*

ART DECO PIECES RE-CREATE A WHOLE

One of the more interesting facets of collecting objects and artifacts from a particular period is the way these possessions can be reintegrated into a new environment. In the most successful situations, the objects are adapted so that they contribute to a new whole, and the collection itself becomes much more evocative than the sum of its parts. Such is the case of a collection of Art Deco furnishings which incorporates rare seating pieces, lighting fixtures, and original hardware, as well as art objects, in a gracious town house in South London.

From the chromed shelving by Pierre Chareau in the study, to the bathroom fixtures that come from the Savoy Hotel, from the columns supporting the hall console table, which were in a now defunct Liverpool cinema house, to the radiator grilles originally designed for the Lloyds of London insurance firm, everything used in the town house is as utilitarian as it is decorative.

ABOVE FAR LEFT: *The glass-covered courtyard of the London town house.*

FAR LEFT: *The wall-hung bookcase system in the study was designed by the 1930s French architect Pierre Chareau.*

ABOVE LEFT: *The legs on the console in the entrance hall were cut down from the glass columns of an old Liverpool movie house.*

LEFT: *The shiny mirrored mantelpiece is reflected in the glass top of the coffee table in the study.*

RIGHT: *The foyer and stairway are dominated by the globe-shaped lighting fixture, an Art Deco prototype by Jallot.*

LEFT: *The double doors that lead from the living room to the hall and the master bedroom have been mirrored on one side.*

BELOW LEFT: *A diamond-shaped mirror hangs above a stainless-steel wall grille in the bedroom.*

RIGHT: *The living room is furnished with Art Deco pieces and includes a Scottish carpet from 1910 attributed to Charles Rennie Mackintosh, a sharkskin daybed by Emile-Jacques Ruhlmann, bronze standing lamps, and a marble console table.*

RECOLLECTION OF AN ERA

The idea was to make the ground floor of an ordinary 1870s terrace house near London's Portobello Road look "as if it had been there forever." Or at least as if it had been there since the 1830s, the "absolute favorite era" of its current occupant, a curator at the Victoria and Albert Museum. According to the creator of the unusual interior, the 1830s was a time when "it seemed natural to mix things of all sorts."

Made up of two large rooms—one based on a red room in Sir John Soane's famous house, the other painted in trompe l'oeil and dedicated to Napoleon's Egyptian campaign—the apartment has been decorated with a collection of 19th-century finds, including a wax model under glass of Queen Victoria, an imposing pair of 18th-century Gothic bookcases, and a very large Regency wardrobe. "I did a lot of looking around," the apartment's designer explained, "and what I couldn't find I made myself."

LEFT: *A wax model of Queen Victoria in her coronation robes and some Egyptian antiquities are displayed under glass domes on a table in the living room.*

BELOW LEFT: *Near the door, above an 1830 Gothic chair, are hung drawings of Gothic stained-glass designs. The door and the light switch have been framed in trompe l'oeil-painted marble.*

RIGHT: *The curtains in the living room were copied from an early-19th-century book on draperies and upholstery. A pair of late-18th-century Gothic bookcases stand in the windows. The table and chairs date from about 1820.*

LEFT AND BELOW LEFT: *A mid-17th-century black cabinet filled with curiosities has been placed at one end of the red living room. A collection of engravings that are not framed but glued to the wall are surrounded by printed borders to give the effect of an 18th-century print room.*

BOTTOM LEFT: *The small fan-shaped guide board, copied from those used in stately homes, is meant to provide a key for the identification of the prints on the wall in the room.*

RIGHT: *A book-covered table sits in the middle of the living room, whose decor was inspired by a room in Sir John Soane's house. The idea was to reproduce an interior that might have belonged to an early-19th-century antiquarian.*

ABOVE: *The faux-marbre fireplace is flanked by two Indian Regency ebony chairs. An antique French gilt clock is centered on the mantel.*

LEFT: *A detail of the mantelpiece painted in trompe l'oeil marble.*

ABOVE: *The blue bedroom was painted in trompe l'oeil and is based on a Napoleonic theme.*

RIGHT: *The modern bed has been draped with diaphanous material to match the pale blue walls.*

ABOVE: *A Chinese carpet covers the floor and a Regency chair is placed near the bed. In the corner is a Regency chest of drawers.*

AN ACCUMULATION OF MEMENTOS

There are some people who simply never throw anything away. And Natalie Gibson, a London-based textile designer, is one of them. For the past 18 years she has lived in a 1650 house near Tower Bridge in South London.

Gibson collects everything from china teapots and the myriad fans she sometimes incorporates into her work to overscale amusement park displays. Her tiny house acts as an always changing backdrop for her mementos. Over the years, she has stripped countless layers of paint off the paneled walls. A wooden dresser, discovered in the street, has become the repository for dozens of her finds.

Recently Jon Wealleans, an architect, has moved into the house, and has started building cupboards. "He's trying to organize me," Gibson said. "But he can't really, because it's just too late."

LEFT: *The china-laden dresser is the focus of the large eat-in kitchen. The shooting star, made of small fairy lights, was originally an Italian Christmas decoration.*

ABOVE LEFT: *Everyday flatware is kept in a drawer of the wood kitchen table. A huge butterfly is fixed onto the wall.*

ABOVE: *A metal peacock that was part of the famous Blackpool illuminations of 1928 has been hung in the stair.*

BELOW: *In the living room area, two pieces by Stephen Buckley are displayed on one wall. The sculpture on the left is by John Duff. The stool and table are Mies van der Rohe designs.*

RIGHT: *A piece by Clarke Murray, an American artist, has been mounted on the circular elevator enclosure and can be seen from the study. A work by Jennifer Bartlett is shown on the wall at the left.*

MODERN ART, CALM SPACE

When Max Gordon, an architect, moved into the top floor of a 100-year-old London house about four years ago, he stripped away all the moldings and took down as many walls as he could with the intention of "making an open, calm, fluent space" that would be a background for his collection of modern English and American art.

At the center of the new flat stands a circular funnel-like structure that contains the building's spiral staircase and round elevator. In relation to the apartment, the curved wall becomes another clean surface against which art can be displayed. The floors are covered in off-white carpeting, and all the upholstered pieces match the carpet in color so as to be perceived as "mounds" rather than as individual pieces.

Lighting was an important consideration. The architect devised a series of sliding, floor-to-ceiling translucent fiberglass panels to diffuse the daylight. For artificial lighting, Gordon installed fluorescent tubes "to light the space rather than the objects." As he explained: "The idea was to avoid conventional art gallery lighting, usually downlighting, that creates harsh shadows."

FAR LEFT: *The round elevator opens directly into the apartment.*

BELOW FAR LEFT: *The doors of the renovated apartment have been curved to follow the shape of the elevator drum enclosure.*

LEFT: *The bedroom area cannot be closed off to the rest of the space. When additional space is needed for parties, a flap in the wall behind the bookcase flips up to provide storage space for the bed in the closet. The large painting over the bed is by Keith Milow; the resin-and-brass piece on the other wall is by Michael Sander.*

BELOW LEFT: *The study includes a desk designed by Max Gordon, a chaise by Le Corbusier, lamps by Richard Sapper, a circular painting by Joe Zucker, and a cross by Keith Milow. The screen at the right is actually a set of folding table leaves.*

ABOVE RIGHT: *Another piece by Joe Zucker has been hung on the curved wall between the bedroom and living room spaces.*

RIGHT: *Ron Gorchov painted the blue piece in the dining area, and the painting of shirts on the left is by Lisa Milroy. Over the windows are hung sliding translucent fiberglass panels that help diffuse the daylight.*

259

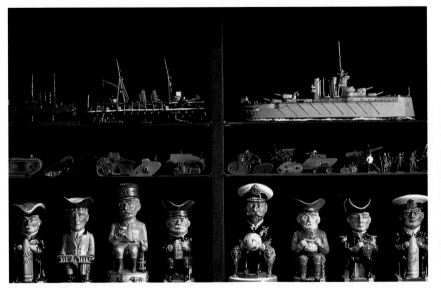
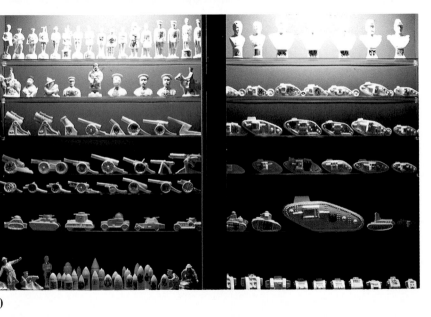

FRONT LINE MEMORABILIA

The late William Gough Howell spent 15 years accumulating his unusual and exhaustive collection of World War I memorabilia. The architect had started with an interest in the period and the popular art of the 1920s and 1930s, spending weekends searching out the objects in junk shops throughout the country and in the antiques shops on London's Portobello Road.

The collection was installed in a gallery in his country house. Among the artifacts are commemorative china, models of war memorials and cathedrals, pincushions, spoons, tin toys, cigarette lighters, Flag Day flags, postcards, posters, toy soldiers, and model boats and airplanes.

TOP FAR LEFT AND TOP LEFT: *The collection of World War I memorabilia includes pins in the shape of airplane propellors, china, mock medals, political campaign buttons, and Flag Day flags.*

ABOVE FAR LEFT: *Commemorative china was often marked with the insignia of a resort town.*

ABOVE LEFT: *Model and toy airplanes were made of wood, brass, or tin.*

FAR LEFT: *A display case holds model boats, miniature tanks, and a row of Toby jugs that portray some of the important personalities of the period.*

LEFT: *White china tanks, guns, and busts are in a vitrine.*

RIGHT: *The collection has been housed in a museumlike setting on the top floor of a country house.*

ENGLISH STYLE ABROAD

Like English manners and English literature, the English design style has always had a particular appeal for those living abroad. And many American interior decorators have made international reputations reinterpreting the English country-house style. This not only includes beautifully patinaed walls, collections of export porcelains, and chintz-upholstered sofas, but also romantic interpretations of feminine bedrooms, dark-paneled libraries, society gentlemen's dressing rooms, and cozy, pine furniture-filled sitting rooms.

The English Tudor-style house on Long Island has a front garden of perennial flowers.

Tiny villa made by Thomas Risley in 1889.

LEFT: *Georgina Fairholme's country bedroom has been decorated in a classical blue-and-white color scheme. The walls are wallpapered, the four-poster bed is covered with a quilt, and trompe l'oeil Delftlike tiles line the fireplace.*

LEFT: *In Tricia Foley's living room, the English theme is carried through with rusticated furniture, blue-and-white china, and delicate old lace.*

TOWN HOUSE, COUNTRY LOOK

"The English look needs a high-ceilinged room," said Mario Buatta, one of the best known of the American interior decorators, who has made his reputation on reinterpreting the style of the English country house.

His oft-photographed New York apartment in a late 1920s Federal-style town house is his calling card. In it he has assembled all the things that are for him the essence of British interiors—or what he described as "a very romantic, colorful look, the feeling of so many things from so many different periods coming together."

Here that mix includes an early-18th-century red lacquer Queen Anne bureau that is filled with lettuce- and cabbage-shaped botanical porcelains and pottery; a collection of dog paintings from the 18th and 19th centuries hung on sashes and bows; glazed walls and trompe l'oeil-painted floors by Robert Jackson; upholstery that is covered with classic chintzes; and a book-laden table in what was once the reception room of the house. There the niches are filled with blue-and-white china that ranges from the 17th century to 1983. The pale cantaloupe-colored walls are set off with white woodwork inspired by those in decorator Nancy Lancaster's Hasley Court house.

FAR LEFT: *A book-laden table with a French faïence stove as its centerpiece stands in the middle of the entrance hall. The walls have been glazed the color of pale cantaloupe and the woodwork painted in different shades of white. The niches are filled with the decorator's blue-and-white china.*

BELOW FAR LEFT: *Antique dog paintings have been hung on sashes against the walnut paneling in the living room that has been glazed in three shades of pistachio green. The floor was painted by Robert Jackson to look like sisal. The furniture is covered with classic chintz fabrics.*

LEFT: *Cabbage-shaped porcelains and pottery and tulip-shaped Spode and Staffordshire chocolate cups are some of the pieces displayed on the red lacquer Queen Anne secretary in the living room.*

HUDSON RIVER FORMAL HOUSE

Upstate New York is an area dotted with historic mansions that overlook the Hudson River. Teviotdale, built in 1773 by Walter Livingston, an important landowner, and later the home of Robert Fulton, the inventor of the steamboat, is one of the finest examples of Georgian houses in the region.

When the residence was bought in 1971 by the late Harrison Cultra and Richard Barker, it had been uninhabited for nearly 40 years. The renovated interior reflects both the mansion's original Georgian style and its English antecedents.

Harrison's idea was to make it look as if a family had always lived there and to keep the setting "very, very 18th century," Barker explained.

It took four months to cut the wood pieces, two months to install, and two months to paint the extravagant Chinese Chippendale staircase. "It was the single most troublesome and expensive thing in the house," Barker admitted, "but it was worth it because it remains as one of Harrison's tours de force."

ABOVE LEFT: *Teviotdale was built of stone rubble covered with stucco.*

LEFT: *In the hall, a basket is filled with an assortment of hats.*

RIGHT: *The Chinese Chippendale staircase and the Chinese lantern were designed by Harrison Cultra. The faux-marbre floor was painted by Robert Jackson.*

ABOVE: *An antique bench stands by the stairway.*

LEFT: *The gold-painted sculpture on a pedestal in the hall is by Rodney Letheridge, a contemporary American artist.*

ABOVE: *The canopied bed is in the master bedroom.*

RIGHT AND BELOW RIGHT: *The library with its blue walls was inspired by one of the house's early occupants, Robert Fulton. The draperies and upholstery are covered in a chintz with a shell pattern that emphasizes the sea motif of the room.*

REVISITED VICTORIANA

The comfortable and eccentric mix of objects that is usually associated with the English country house has found its American equivalent in Keith and Chippy Irvine's upstate New York farmhouse.

"It's all a muddle," said the Scottish-born interior designer, who with his English wife has in the last 15 years filled the 1870s Victorian house with family heirlooms, an early Georgian table, an English Hepplewhite chair, American rattan sofas, the throne on which Vivien Leigh sat when she played Cleopatra, lots of nicely faded chintz, late-19th-century Royal Family Staffordshire pottery, and a few pieces left to Irvine by John Fowler, for whom he worked in the 1950s.

ABOVE FAR LEFT: *The furnishings in the winter sitting room include an early-18th-century walnut cabinet, a chintz-covered sofa, and an English Hepplewhite chair slipcovered in toile.*

FAR LEFT: *Beyond the white-painted front gate can be glimpsed the Victorian farmhouse in upstate New York that belongs to Keith and Chippy Irvine.*

LEFT: *A hollyhock grows through a painted wire seat in the garden.*

ABOVE: *The walls of the library are papered in a tartan plaid. A chintz with roses and whippets has been used for the draperies and some of the furniture. The coffee table is a Scottish butler's tray.*

ABOVE: *Red velvet curtains are hung in the doorway of the dining room to keep out drafts.*

LEFT: *The winter drawing room was put together from bits and pieces collected over the years by the Irvines. The screen is made from a series of antique wallpaper panels.*

LEFT: *The table is conveniently set near the fireplace. Most of the 17th- and 18th-century furniture is of English oak. The picture above the mantel is a contemporary portrait of Mr. Irvine as Mary Queen of Scots.*

ABOVE: *An antique rack by the piano holds a collection of hats. The color of the lace curtains was obtained by dipping them in coffee.*

RIGHT: *Antique chintz has been lined to match the fabric used on the bed canopy in the guest room. An American quilt covers the bed.*

RIGHT: *A late-19th-century American mahogany canopy bed takes up most of the master bedroom. The walls are covered with a Victorian document paper.*

LEFT: *On Shelter Island, N.Y., an old-fashioned garden seat is surrounded by trees in a luxuriant garden that is evocative of many bucolic English sites.*

JOHN LIDGETT and SONS' LINE OF AUSTRALIAN PACKET SHIPS.—For PORT PHILLIP, the LOCH CASTLE; that ship is expected to sail in a few tons of light measurement at the London Dock Jetty; for freight of which apply to John Lidgett and Sons, 9, Billiter-street.

STEAM to AUSTRALIA.—The Tasmanian Steam Navigation Company's beautiful new iron screw steam ship CITY of HOBART, 813 tons and upwards, will be despatched punctually on March 27, for MELBOURNE, Port Phillip, calling at Hobart Town to land passengers, &c., commanded by Captain JOHN THOM, so well known to most persons connected with Australia.

EMPERANCE LINE OF PACKETS, from London to Australia.—Arrival of the ship California.

NOR HOBART TOWN, has just delivered her inward cargo in first-rate order, and will return immediately.

NEW ZEALAND.—Notice to Shippers per NORMAN MORRISON.—All goods intended for shipment by this vessel must be alongside and cleared on the morning of the 25th.

NOR NEW YORK, to sail on the 25th of February the splendid, fast-sailing, first-class American packet ship RICHARD COBDEN, A 1, burden 1,000 tons, coppered and copperfastened, GEORGE BARRELL, Commander.

STEAM to NEW YORK—UNITED STATES MAIL STEAMERS will leave Southampton for NEW YORK as follows.

STEAM to AMERICA.—The Liverpool and Philadelphia Steam Ship Company intend to despatch their favourite screw steam ships from Liverpool to Philadelphia.

STEAM to NEW YORK.—THE UNITED STATES MAIL STEAMERS—ATLANTIC, Captain WEST; PACIFIC, Captain NYE; ARCTIC, Captain LUCE; BALTIC, Captain COMSTOCK—are appointed to sail fortnightly, as under:—
From Liverpool.
ATLANTIC, Wednesday, February 22.
PACIFIC, Wednesday, March 8.

W. S. W., who LEFT his HOME on Saturday, the 4th inst., purposing to go to Brighton, is requested to COMMUNICATE with his friends, who are anxious to hear from him.

LOST, on Saturday, in the vicinity of Coveat-garden, a SCOTCH TERRIER PUP; answers to the name of "Jem." Colour sandy. FIVE SHILLINGS REWARD will be given if returned to 100, Strand.

LOST, in the Regent's-park, on Saturday evening, Feb. 18th, a SLATE-COLOURED ISLE of SKYE TERRIER, with collar, inscribed Lady Anne Dashwood, 9, Seamore-place, Mayfair. Whoever brings him to the above address will receive TWO POUNDS REWARD.

TWENTY SHILLINGS REWARD.—LOST, on Feb. 13, in the Goswell road, a rough WHITE TERRIER DOG, cropped right ear tipped with black, on the left a bar of black, black and white nose white roof.

ELIZABETH JAMES, living, a widow, in the parish of St. Mary, Lambeth, county of Surrey. In 1776, her DESCENDANT and HEIR, or Legal Representative, will HEAR of SOMETHING to his or her ADVANTAGE.

THE HEIRS or NEXT of KIN of JOHN KENWORTHY, of Ironmonger-lane, Manchester warehouseman, and of JOHN CHORLEY, of Gracechurch-street, linendraper, both in the city of London.

WANTED, of ELIZ— 60 in 1775, when a—Wild street, Lin—Siddon, of Manch—to Mr. Moreland—to Mr. James M.

OPERA-—landing of E—barrelled BLACK—satin. Whoever r—49, Parliament-st.

FOUND, on Ealing co—land-wharf, 8, ran—

IF DAVID—Brighton, Sussex—road, Dalston, he—

RAMSGA—GEORGE —with their friends—their ADVANTA—

IF the PRO—Fitzroy-squa—and New Fortman—not REDEEMED—to pay expenses.

THE Gene—class STEA—EDINBURGH—

NEWCASTLE—HULL.—Every—YARMOUTH—Offices, 71, Lom—

DUNDEE.—Reduced f—second cabin, 26s—second cabin, 15s—lin's, Regent-cir—Downe's-wharf.

ABERDEEN STEAM NAVIGATION COMPANY.—This Company's splendid and powerful steam ships will start from the Aberdeen Steam-wharf, 257, Wapping, as under, weather, &c., permitting:—
For ABERDEEN, the EARL of ABERDEEN, Wednesday, Feb. 2, at 12 noon, taking goods for Stonehaven, Montrose, Peterhead, Banff, Burghead, Cromarty, Invergordon, Chanonry Point, Inverness, and all the north of Scotland.

STEAM to DUBLIN, calling at Southampton, Plymouth, and Falmouth.—The British and Irish Steam Packet Company's steamer CITY of LIMERICK, Capt. W. BISHOP, will sail from off the British and Foreign and Dublin, Belfast, Cork, and Limerick Steam-wharf, Lower East Smithfield.

YACHT for SALE, cutter-rigged, and in excellent condition; sails nearly new. For particulars and to see the same apply to John Middleton, Cookham, near Maidenhead, Berks.

YACHT WANTED, to PURCHASE, from 30 to 35 or 40 tons or so. She must be a modern, carvel-built vessel, copper and copper-fastened.

THE very superior new American ship RED JACKET, now lying at Liverpool, recently arrived from New York, on her first voyage, after an unparalleled passage of 13 days.

ADAMS'S ANNUAL BALL.—Mr. THOMAS ADAMS has the honour to announce to his numerous patrons that his EIGHTEENTH ANNUAL BALL will take place at Willis's Rooms, King-street, St. James's, THIS EVENING.

HON. ARTILLERY COMPANY'S BALL.—Police Regulations for the Arrangement of Carriages at the Artillery Ground, City-road, this day, Feb. 21.

PORTLAND ROOMS, Foley-place.—Miss EMMA HONEY, of the Theatre Royal Drury-lane, begs to announce that her FULL DRESS BALL will take place at the above Rooms, on Monday, the 27th inst.

MR. ALBERT SMITH'S MONT BLANC (including the Bernese Oberland and the Simplon), every evening at 8 o'clock (except Saturday); and Tuesday, Thursday, and Saturday mornings, at 3. Stalls 3s., which can be taken at the box-office.

WILL SHORTLY CLOSE.—J. R. SMITH'S GRAND TOUR OF EUROPE and ASCENT of MONT BLANC, now OPEN daily, at 3 and 8 o'clock, at Leicester-square.

W. S. WOODIN'S CARPET-BAG and SKETCH-BOOK, Upper Hall, Regent Gallery, every evening at 8 o'clock.

THE HIBERNIA will SHORTLY CLOSE.—Mrs. GIBB'S IRISH ENTERTAINMENT, the "Emerald Isle" and "Lakes of Killarney," at the Hibernia, 309, Regent-street, next the Polytechnic, every evening, at 8; mornings, Mondays, Wednesdays, and Saturdays, at 3.

PHOTOGRAPHIC SOCIETY.—The EXHIBITION of PHOTOGRAPHS and DAGUERREOTYPES is now OPEN at the Gallery of British Artists, Suffolk-street, Pall-mall, in the morning, from 10 a.m. to half-past 4 p.m.

EGYPTIAN HALL.—CONSTANTINOPLE

THE most INTERESTING GROUP ever MODELLED.—Her Majesty the Queen, H.R.H. Prince Albert, Prince of Wales, Prince Alfred, Princess Royal, the Princesses Alice, Helena, Louisa, &c., honoured with the highest encomiums.—Madame TUSSAUD and SONS' EXHIBITION, Bazaar, Baker-street.

ZOOLOGICAL GARDENS, Regent's-park.—Fellows and visitors are informed that a specimen of the Giant Anteater and an adult pair of Indian Lions have been added to the Collection.

MR. CALDWELL'S ANNUAL FULL-DRESS BALL will take place THIS EVENING, Feb. 21st.

A very light cab-headed DENNET, on high wheels, Collinge's axles, £25.

A New, elegant, circular-fronted BASTERNA BROUGHAM, painted lake.

TO be SOLD, a bargain, a CAB PHAETON.

PONY PHAETON for SALE, the property of an invalid gentleman.

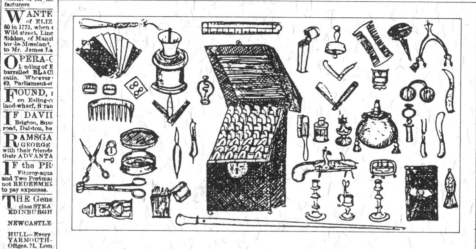

CATALOGUE OF SOURCES

SACRED HARMONIC SOCIETY, Exeter-hall.—Conductor—Mr. COSTA—Friday next, February 24, HAYDN'S CREATION. Vocalists—Miss Birch, Mrs. Sims Reeves, Mr. J. W. Bradbury, and Signor Belletti, with orchestra of 700 performers. Tickets 3s., 5s., and 10s. 6d. each.

HARMONIC UNION, Exeter-hall.—Conductor Mr. BENEDICT.—HANDEL'S ACIS and GALATEA with Mozart's accompaniments, and Mendelssohn's Music to a Midsummer's Night's Dream. Vocalists—Miss Stabbach, Miss Thirlwall, Mr. Sims Reeves, Mr. S. Champion, and Signor Belletti.

IMMANUEL, the NEW ORATORIO, by Mr. HENRY LESLIE.—The FIRST PERFORMANCE will be given at St. Martin's-hall, on Thursday, March 2, for the Benefit of the Governesses' Benevolent Institution.

ST. MARTIN'S-HALL.—Miss BIRCH has the honour to announce that her GRAND BENEFIT CONCERT, with orchestra complete in every department, will be given on this evening, Tuesday, March 28, under the direction of Mr. John Hullah.

N's-HALL.—HANDEL'S JUDAS will be performed on Wednesday next, Feb. 22, Mr. JOHN HULLAH. Principal vocalists.

's HALL.—Judas Maccabeus.—of the WORDS, 6d. each, to be had only at the hall on the evening of performance.

RRAS has the honour to announce DE MATINEE MUSICALE will take place on at the Dudley Gallery (by the kind permission of Lord Ward), when a selection from Verdi's new music.

REEVES, Mlle. Graver, and a host Instrumental Talent, at the WEDNESDAY CONCERTS, Exeter-hall, on the 22d (To-morrow).

REEVES will appear THIS EVENING SIXTH CONCERT of the St. JOHN'S-WOOD PRESS CONCERTS, at the Eyre Arms Concert-room.

RNDALE BENNETT respectfully the Second of his TENTH ANNUAL SERIES of CLASSICAL PIANOFORTE MUSIC.

EDNEY'S MUSICAL LECTURES AINMENTS.—Mr. JOHN EDNEY is honoured SING and LECTURE at the THIS EVENING, Feb. 21st; Hampton, 27th.

HUNGARIAN CONCERTS: 8 to 10. Admission 1s.—The greatest musical treat in London may be enjoyed every evening at the Royal Marionette Theatre, where the renowned HUNGARIAN BAND instrumentalists, in the most effective style.

MR. J. E. CARPENTER will give his popular ENTERTAINMENT—"The Road, the River, and the Rail"—assisted by Miss Jolly, at Cheltenham, Feb. 23, 24, and 25; Stroud, 27 and 28; Stourbridge, March 3, &c.—7, Mildmay Villas, Kingsland.

LOVE in a NEW ENTERTAINMENT.—Horns, Kennington.—THIS EVENING, Feb. 21, Mr. Love will appear at the Horns, Kennington.

GREAT GLOBE, Leicester-square.—Turkey in Europe.—LECTURES on the GEOGRAPHY of TURKEY in Europe and Asia.

THE ESQUIMAUX FAMILY, from Cumberland Straits, having had the honour of appearing, by Royal Command, before Her Most Gracious Majesty the Queen, at Windsor Castle, will be EXHIBITED at the Lowther-arcade Exhibition Rooms.

TO be SOLD, price £20, ING, four years old, 14 hands to ride or drive. Any reasonable trial 6, Tyers-street, Lambeth.

HORSES.—Notice.—No having HORSES to dispose CHASERS for them by applying at Horses, Carriage, &c.

PONY, Harness, and Bas others for SALE and to order, Albert Day Pim's stables, street-road, where may be seen to Railway Car, adapted for country.

A BARGAIN—GRAY C half its value, the property of five years old, rides remarkably we accustomed to go in 4-wheel chaise Horse livery stables, Curtain road.

A TEAM of FOUR CA CART HORSES for SALE, at R. A. S. Gloucester Prize, 15s.

TWO PAIR of BAY HOR hands 2 inches high, 5 years old 16 hands high, six years old; fine lady. Can be examined. Apply to Mr Gutteridge, 8, L.

CHILD'S PONIES.—A PONY, six years old, and a Gray under tax, quiet with children, and make a good match in harness.

TO be SOLD (the property may be ref rred to), a pout also a Brown Mare, 14 hands.

ONE of strongest COB P hands high, a perfect dray horse new Albert Phaeton, to carry four.

IRISH HORSES on SALE property of a gentleman, consign very superior Bay Gelding.

TWO CART HORSES, 7 less, taken under an execution TION, without reserve, by Mr. F. MA Smith's-lane, To-morrow (Wednesday).

ALDRIDGE'S.—To be SO Mr. F. MATTAM, at Aldridge's (Wednesday), February 22.

ALDRIDGE'S.—To be SO Mr. F. MATTAM, at Aldridge's (Wednesday), Feb. 22, the property MARE.

ALDRIDGE'S.—The publ quested to take notice, that the continued to sales by auction and comm no any direct or indirect patronage.

ALDRIDGE'S.—EIGHTEEN HORSES (being the Horses, &c., will be SOLD by AUCT Aldridge's, St. Martin's-lane, To-morro at 12 precisely.

TWENTY ENGLISH HORSES.—To be SOLD by AUCT Little Britain, on Thursday, February 23, powerful, active, seasoned ENGLISH an direct from work.

TWELVE superior good-si To be SOLD by AUCTION a Britain, city, on Tuesday, February known, good seasoned HORSES.

ONE HUNDRED and FO POSITORY.—Messrs. RYMIL SOLD by AUCTION, Mr. Messrs. RYMIL repository, Barbican, on Friday next.

ENGLISH and BELGIUM City Repository, Barbican.—Messrs. now on view, and SALE by private con short-legged, English and Belgian CAR.

IRISH HACKS, Hunters, Messrs. RYMILL and GOWER have Hennessey to SELL by AUCTION, at F Friday, Feb. 24, his second consignment.

Antique furniture and collectibles are among the most popular of English exports. But the English look also involves reproduction furniture, fabrics and wall coverings, housewares, and garden furnishings. We have tried to include a wide range of shops that deal in English wares. The major department stores in large cities often run promotions on English themes and are also a good source.

The symbol R stands for retailer, W for wholesaler or importer, and MO for mail order. When a retail store or wholesale showroom has more than one location, we have listed the main store first, then the others in alphabetical order. It is often useful to write to a wholesaler and request a list of the shops in your area to which they distribute their products.

Every effort has been made to be complete and accurate. If some sources have not been included and some addresses have changed, we will try to make the necessary corrections in future printings.

ANTIQUES

DON BADERTSCHER IMPORTS
716 North La Cienega Blvd.
Los Angeles, Calif. 90069
(213)655-6448
Late 19th- early 20th-century dressers, sideboards, overmantels, fireplaces, garden furniture, and kitchen accessories. (R) (W)

BALASSES HOUSE ANTIQUES
Main St.
Amagansett, N.Y. 11930
(516)267-3032
English country furniture, including pine farm tables, corner cupboards, and sideboards; Windsor chairs, brass lamps, and hanging light fixtures, accessories, and antique kitchenware. (R)

English china and glass, Bardith Ltd.

BARDITH LTD.
901 Madison Ave.
New York, N.Y. 10021
(212)737-3775
Complete antique dinner, tea and dessert sets, tureens, cachepots, plates, cups, bowls, and platters in fine English china, including Wedgwood, Spode, Derby, pearlware, and delftware; 19th-century papier-mâché trays; antique brass and glass hanging light fixtures; old glass dishes, decanters, and glasses. (R) (T)

BARNEYS NEW YORK
106 Seventh Ave.
New York, N.Y. 10011
(212)929-9000
Antique tea sets, dinnerware, and vases by Clarice Cliff and Susie Cooper and Shelley porcelain; antique silver picture frames, and serving pieces. (R)

MIKE BELL ANTIQUE SHOWROOMS
60 East 10th St.
New York, N.Y. 10003
(212)598-4677

12110 Merchandise Mart
Chicago, Ill. 60654
(312)661-7099

Eighteenth- and 19th-century stripped pine country furniture, including bookcases, armoires, and tables; new pieces from old wood and architectural remnants. (T)

BRITISH COUNTRY ANTIQUES
50 Main St. North
Woodbury, Conn. 06798
(203)263-5100
Eighteenth- and 19th-century polished pine country furniture; accessories including Victorian biscuit barrels, boxes in oak and silver, turned wood objects, majolica, and blue-and-white earthenware. (R) (T)

R. BROOKE LTD.
138½ East 80th St.
New York, N.Y. 10028
(212)535-0707
Eighteenth- and 19th-century furniture; accessories in porcelain, silver, and tortoiseshell; prints, drawings, and collectibles. (R) (T)

BULL AND BEAR ANTIQUES
1189 Howell Mill Rd., N.W.
Atlanta, Ga. 30318
(404)355-6697
Eighteenth-century furniture; Staffordshire figures. (R)

RICHARD CAMP
Montauk Highway
Wainscott, N.Y. 11975
(516)537-0330
Platters, bowls, vases, and English commemorative memorabilia; bamboo and pine furniture; Lloyd Loom chairs. (R) (T)

PHILIP COLLECK OF LONDON LTD.
830 Broadway
New York, N.Y. 10003
(212)505-2500
Queen Anne, Chippendale, Adam, Hepplewhite, and Regency antique furniture; paintings, lacquerware, porcelain, screens, accessories, and mirrors. (R) (T)

ENGLISH HERITAGE
8424 Melrose Pl.
Los Angeles, Calif. 90069
(213)655-5946
Country and formal furniture, including yewwood desks, tables, and corner cabinets; fine Georgian silver. (R) (T)

ENGLISH HERITAGE ANTIQUES, INC.
13 South Ave.
New Canaan, Conn. 06840
(203)966-2979
Formal 18th- and 19th-century furniture, porcelain, brass, and silver. (R)

FALLEN OAKS LTD.
1075 Gage St.
Winnetka, Ill. 60093
(312)446-3540
Sixteenth- and 17th-century oak furniture, especially Tudor pieces; tapestries, brass, and metalware, paintings, wood and stone carvings, and textiles from the period. (R) (T)

RUFUS FOSHEE ANTIQUES
P.O. Box 839
Camden, Maine 04843
(207)236-2838
Eighteenth- and 19th-century pottery and porcelain, including Delftware, creamware, and pearlware; majolica, spatterware, and spongeware. (R) (T)

MALCOLM FRANKLIN, INC.
15 East 57th St.
New York, N.Y. 10022
(212)308-3344

126 East Delaware Pl.
Chicago, Ill. 60611
(312)337-0202
Fine 18th-century furniture and accessories, including clocks and mirrors. (R) (T)

GREAT BRAMPTON HOUSE ANTIQUES (AMERICA), INC.
163 Turn of River Rd.
Stamford, Conn. 06905
(203)322-8581
Fine antique furniture, including large dining tables, chairs, mirrors, and four-poster beds. (R) (T) By appointment only.

HAMILTON-HYRE LTD.
413 Bleecker St.
New York, N.Y. 10014
(212)989-4509
Eighteenth-, 19th-, and early 20th-century furniture and accessories, especially faux bamboo and painted furniture; majolica. (R) (T)

HARWOOD GALLERIES
1045 Madison Ave.
New York, N.Y. 10021
(212)744-5062
Late 19th- and early 20th-century bentwood tables and chairs by Thonet and J. J. Kohn; English Arts and Crafts pottery by Moorcroft, Minton, and Royal Doulton. (R)

HYDE PARK ANTIQUES LTD.
836 Broadway
New York, N.Y. 10003
(212)477-0033
Regency furniture and fine 18th- and 19th-century formal furniture; porcelain, mirrors, and sporting paintings. (R) (T)

JACKSON-MITCHELL, INC.
412 Delaware St.
New Castle, Del. 19720
(302)322-4363
Seventeenth-, 18th-, and early 19th-century English formal and

Birdcages, tables, and lights, Ann Morris Antiques, Inc.

country furniture and objects; 17th- and 18th-century brass and copper and 19th-century decorative metalware, including copper jelly molds. (R)*

JAMES II GALLERIES, INC.
15 East 57th St.
New York, N.Y. 10022
(212)355-7040
Collections of picture frames, walking canes, ivory, glass of all periods, silver and silver plate, papier-mâché, pottery and porcelain, miniatures, pillboxes, and candlesticks; some furniture, including hat stands, small chairs, and bamboo pieces. (R)

KENSINGTON PLACE ANTIQUES
80 East 11th St.
New York, N.Y. 10003
(212)533-7652
Fine 18th- and 19th-century decorative furniture and objects; period prints a specialty. (R) (T)

KENTSHIRE GALLERIES LTD.
37 East 12th St.
New York, N.Y. 10003
(212)673-6644
Regency and large-scale formal

mahogany and pine furniture, including breakfronts, partner's desks, and writing tables, 19th-century sporting paintings, vases, boxes, candlesticks, and lighting fixtures. (T) (W)*

KNOCK ON WOOD, INC.
1078-R Post Rd.
Darien, Conn. 06820
(203)655-9031
Polished pine, oak, and mahogany country furniture; antique kitchenware and copper and brass accessories. (T) (W)

LA COMPAGNIE ANGLAISE, INC.
1113 Madison Ave.
New York, N.Y. 10028
(212)772-8515
Refinished country furniture in hardwoods and pine, including dressers, tables, chests, and mantels. (R) (T)

LINLO HOUSE, INC.
1019 Lexington Ave.
New York, N.Y. 10021
(212)288-1848
Eighteenth- and early 19th-century furniture, including oak chests, dressers, and desks; porcelain, lighting fixtures, and prints. (R) (T)

DIANE LOVE, INC.
851 Madison Ave.
New York, N.Y. 10021
(212)879-6997
English Arts and Crafts furniture; bentwood, bamboo, and Lloyd Loom pieces; art pottery, including Clarice Cliff and Shelley designs; pewter and silver designed by Archibald Knox for Liberty & Co., London. (R) (W)

J. GARVIN MECKING, INC.
188 East 64th St.
New York, N.Y. 10021
(212)688-0840
Decorative accessories and furniture from all periods, including antique needlepoint, majolica, lacquerware, papier-mâché, tole, treen, and objects with animal motifs; bamboo and twig furniture. (R) (T)

SUSAN P. MEISEL
133 Prince St.
New York, N.Y. 10012
(212)254-0137
Clarice Cliff 1928–35 pottery; antique toys. (R)

MILL HOUSE ANTIQUES
Route 6
Woodbury, Conn. 06798
(203)263-3446
Eighteenth- and 19th-century furniture in walnut, pine, and mahogany; Welsh dressers, huntboards, and desks. (R) (T)

ANN MORRIS ANTIQUES, INC.
239 East 60th St.
New York, N.Y. 10022
(212)755-3308
Large cabinets, dressers, shop cases, tables, garden benches, apothecary cabinets and jars, pub mirrors, nautical lights, telescopes, and kitchen crockery. (T)

NEWEL ART GALLERIES, INC.
425 East 53rd St.
New York, N.Y. 10022
(212)758-1970
Furniture and objects from the Renaissance to Art Deco periods,

including fine English Adam pieces, Chinese Chippendale breakfronts, mirrors, Brighton Pavilion bamboo and lacquer pieces, hunt tables, large-scale desks, secretaries, chairs, and tables; Victorian wicker, bamboo, and garden furniture; lamps, mirrors, children's chairs, vases, and other accessories. (T)

FLORIAN PAPP, INC.
962 Madison Ave.
New York, N.Y. 10021
(212)288-6770
Fine 18th- and 19th-century furniture, porcelain, chandeliers, clocks, and other accessories.(R)(W)

PHILIP W. PFEIFER
900 Madison Ave.
New York, N.Y. 10021
(212)249-4889
Collections of corkscrews, smoking accessories, pillboxes, walking canes, seals, medical and scientific instruments, games, candlesticks, measuring tools, barometers, and locks. (R)

JUAN PORTELA ANTIQUES
783 Madison Ave.
New York, N.Y. 10021
(212)650-0085
Rare 19th-century furniture, including large-scale secretaries, desks, and tables, inlaid mother-of-pearl and ivory pieces, fine lacquer pieces, and English carpet chairs and sofas; needlepoint rugs, antique silks, and tapestries. (R)

TREVOR POTTS ANTIQUES, INC.
1011 Lexington Ave.
New York, N.Y. 10021
(212)737-0909
Eighteenth- and 19th-century furniture and decorative objects; painted Regency furniture, bamboo pieces, lacquer cabinets and chests; papier-mâché accessories, porcelain, dog paintings, needlework pillows, and carpets. (R) (T)

RALF'S ANTIQUES
807 La Cienega Blvd.
Los Angeles, Calif. 90069

Furniture and decorative objects, Trevor Potts Antiques, Inc.

(213)659-1966
Seventeenth- and 18th-century country furniture; paintings, copper and brass accessories; bronze figurines. (R) (W)

G. RANDALL, INC.
229 North Royal St.
Alexandria, Va. 22314
(212)549-4432
Fine late 17th- and 18th-century furniture, paintings, mirrors, silver, and porcelain. (R) (T)

ALAN Y. ROBERTS, INC.
Scotts Corners
Pound Ridge, N.Y. 10576
(914)764-5427
Queen Anne, Chippendale, Hepplewhite, and Sheraton antique furniture; dining tables and sets of chairs; antique clocks, mirrors, and paintings. (R) (W)

JAMES ROBINSON, INC.
15 East 57th St.
New York, N.Y. 10022
(212)752-6166
Antique silver from the Elizabethan period to George IV, including sets of cutlery, tea and coffee sets, serving pieces, and candlesticks; George III dessert, tea, and dinner services in fine china; English and

Irish glassware of George III period. (R) (T)

MAYA SCHAPER
239 Columbus Ave.
New York, N.Y. 10023
(212)874-7674
Antique kitchenware, including covered china cheese dishes, bowls, breadboards, platters, cutlery, and mugs; antique picture frames and small accessories. (R)

S. J. SHRUBSOLE CORP.
104 East 57th St.
New York, N.Y. 10022
(212)753-8920
Fine antique silver trays, candlesticks, serving pieces, and complete sets of cutlery; old Sheffield plate objects; reproduction flatware in sterling silver. (R)

MALVINA SOLOMON, INC.
1122 Madison Ave.
New York, N.Y. 10028
(212)535-5200
English Arts and Crafts pottery; American and English ceramic tiles, c. 1880–1900. (R) (W)

STAIR & CO.
59 East 57th St.
New York, N.Y. 10022

(212)355-7620
Fine 17th- and 18th-century antiques, including furniture, paintings, Chinese export porcelain, and works of art. (R) (T) (W)

STAIR'S INCURABLE COLLECTOR
42 East 57th St.
New York, N.Y. 10022
(212)755-0140
Regency furniture, 18th- and 19th-century paintings, English and Oriental screens, coffee tables, and lamps. (R) (T) (W)

THE ENGLISH WAY
115 East 60th St.
New York, N.Y. 10022
(212)308-6119

37 Bridge St.
Brooklyn, N.Y. 11201
(212)625-3463

River Bend Dr.
Charlottesville, Va. 22901
(804)977-3952

1361 Bennett Dr.
Langwood, Fla. 32750
(305)331-6217

329 Park Ave. South
Winter Park, Fla. 32789
(305)628-0993

Trade Showroom at
A.D.A.C., Atlanta, Ga. 30305
(404)262-1718
Eighteenth- and 19th-century pine furniture; Lloyd Loom and wicker pieces; antique lace and linens; antique English china and accessories. (R) (T)

TRANQUIL CORNERS ANTIQUES
5634 Chapel Hill Blvd.
Durham, N.C. 27707
(919)489-8362
Eighteenth- and 19th-century furniture and accessories, including Sheffield and sterling silver flatware, trays, and tea sets. (R) (W)

GENE TYSON, INC.
19 East 69th St.
New York, N.Y. 10021
(212)744-5785

Fine 18th-century English furniture, specializing in Regency lacquer and gilded pieces; period mirrors. (R) (T)

EARLE D. VANDEKAR
15 East 57th St.
New York, N.Y. 10022
(212)308-2022
Fine 18th- and 19th-century ceramics, porcelain, pottery, and delftware; Chinese export porcelain; decorative objects. (R) (T)

VERNAY & JUSSEL, INC.
825 Madison Ave.
New York, N.Y. 10021
(212)879-3344
Fine 17th- to 19th-century furniture; pewter, pottery, and brass accessories; English clocks and works of art. (R) (T)

WINDSOR ANTIQUES
1312 Post Rd.
Fairfield, Conn. 06430
(203)255-0056
Country furniture, including dressers, cupboards, and Windsor and ladderback chairs; brass accessories and English earthenware. (R)

YEAKEL VON ELDIK & PRUYN
425 Via Corta
Malaga Colve Plaza
Palos Verdes Estates, Calif. 90274
(213)544-2514
Sixteenth-, 17th-, and 18th-century furniture, including Jacobean, William and Mary, Queen Anne, Chippendale, and Georgian pieces; Chinese porcelain and earthenware, silver, and paintings. (R) (T)

CONTEMPORARY FURNITURE

ATELIER INTERNATIONAL LTD.
595 Madison Ave.
New York, N.Y. 10022
(212)644-0400

Wood and metal tubular furniture, Conran's

Furniture by Charles Rennie Mackintosh and other designers; lamps. (T)

BAKER, KNAPP & TUBBS
200 Lexington Ave.
New York, N.Y. 10016
(212)599-4300
Showrooms also in Atlanta; Beechwood, Oh.; Chicago; Dallas; Grand Rapids, Mich.; High Point, N.C.; Los Angeles; Miami; Philadelphia; San Francisco; and Troy, Mich.; and available in department stores. Call (616)361-7321 for information.
Reproduction furniture from all periods, including Stately Homes collection; tables, chairs, consoles, chests, lacquer cabinets, four-poster beds, and card tables. (T)

BEYLERIAN LTD.
305 East 63rd St.
New York, N.Y. 10021
(212)755-6303
Reproductions of Eileen Gray designs, including sofas, tables, and chairs. (T)

BLAIR HOUSE LTD.
200 Lexington Ave.
New York, N.Y. 10016

(212)889-5500
Rebuilt pine and oak refectory tables, wake tables, chairs, dressers, and partner's desks. (T)

BLATT BILLIARDS
809 Broadway
New York, N.Y. 10003
(213)674-8855
Vintage and new billiards, pool, and snooker tables. (R) (T)

THE BOMBAY COMPANY
P.O. Box 79186
Fort Worth, Tex. 76179
(817)232-5650 in Texas or 1-800-535-6876 for mail-order information and locations of stores in Connecticut; Georgia; Louisiana; Maryland; Massachusetts; New Jersey; Pennsylvania; Tennessee; Washington, D.C.; Virginia; and Texas.
Inexpensive reproduction tea tables, side tables, consoles, butler's tables, library steps, magazine racks, and other small pieces; brass lighting fixtures, candlesticks, lanterns, and compasses. (R) (MO)

YALE R. BURGE REPRODUCTIONS, INC.
305 East 63rd St.

New York, N.Y. 10021
(212)838-4005
Also available at Paul B. Raulet, Atlanta; R. J. Randolph, Inc., Chicago; John Edward Hughes, Inc., Dallas and Houston; Donghia Showrooms, Inc., Los Angeles and Miami; Shears & Window, Denver and San Francisco.
Exact reproductions of Chippendale, Sheraton, Regency, and Georgian tables, chairs, and consoles; also original 18th- and 19th-century antiques. (T)

CLASSIC GALLERY
120 Thompson St.
New York, N.Y. 10012
(212)925-7340
Reproductions of 1930s furniture by P.E.L. Ltd; ceramics, glass, and chrome objects from 1920 to 1930. (R) (T) (W)

CONRAN'S
160 East 54th St.
New York, N.Y. 10022
(212)371-2225

Stores also in Fairfax, Va.; Georgetown, Washington, D.C.; Hackensack, N.J.; King of Prussia, Pa.; Manhasset, N.Y.; New Rochelle, N.Y.; and Willow Grove, Pa.

Mail order only:
145 Huguenot St.
New Rochelle, N.Y. 10801
(914)632-0515 in N.Y. State
(800)431-2718 out of N.Y. State
Upholstered club chairs; oversized sofas; Chesterfield sofas; leather seating; knockdown kits in pine and laminate for storage systems, bookshelves, bedroom sets, children's bunk beds, nursery furniture, tables, trolleys, and complete kitchen systems; metal tubular furniture for tables, chairs, modern and Victorian-style beds, rolling carts, 1950s-style chairs and tables; modern Lloyd Loom wicker chairs, rattan seating, pine chairs, Windsor chairs, and adaptations of Rietveld lacquer and canvas chairs. (R) (MO)

CRATE AND BARREL
1045 Massachusetts Ave.
Cambridge, Mass. 02138
(617)547-3994
Contemporary pine and metal tubular furniture; Windsor and ladderback chairs; trestle tables. (R)

FIFTY/50
793 Broadway
New York, N.Y. 10003
(212)777-3208
Postwar furniture and objects; designs by Alvar Aalto, Charles Eames, Isamu Noguchi, George Nelson, and Frank Lloyd Wright. (R)

FURNITURE OF THE TWENTIETH CENTURY, INC.
227 West 17th St.
New York, N.Y. 10011
(212)929-6023
Reproductions of Eileen Gray furniture, including the Transat chair. (T)

ICF, INC.
305 East 63rd St.
New York, N.Y. 10021
(212)750-0900
Reproduction furniture by Alvar Aalto and Josef Hoffmann; O.M.K. chair and table by Rodney Kinsman. (T) (W)

KPS, INC.
200 Lexington Ave.
New York, N.Y. 10016
(212)686-7784
Reproduction furniture in Queen Anne, Chippendale, Sheraton, Regency, and Hepplewhite styles in mahogany and burl woods, including Regency japanned chairs, harvest tables, dining tables, and breakfronts.

JACK LENOR LARSEN, INC.
232 East 59th St.
New York, N.Y. 10022
(212)674-3993
Available also in J.J.L. showrooms in Chicago, Dallas, Houston, Los Angeles, San Francisco, and Washington, D.C.
Contemporary Larsen Loom chairs in the style of Lloyd Loom. (T)

Fabrics, wall coverings, and borders, Laura Ashley

MANOR HOUSE LTD.
200 Lexington Ave.
New York, N.Y. 10016
(212)532-1127
Reproductions of elm and ash Windsor chairs, ladderback chairs, and refectory tables; Regency and Hepplewhite furniture, hand-painted chests; antique tables, chairs, dressers, and cabinets in oak, pine, and mahogany. (T)

MODERNAGE
795 Broadway
New York, N.Y. 10003
(212)674-5603
Post-1920s designer furniture and objects; handmade rugs, appliquéd cushions, etched glass, and mirrors to order. (R) (T)

ALAN MOSS LTD.
88 Wooster St.
New York, N.Y. 10012
(212)219-1663
Twentieth-century decorative art; Art Deco, postwar, and 1950s and 1960s furniture and objects. (R)(T)

L. CLARK NININGER & CO.
439 Washington Rd.
Woodbury, Conn., 06798
(203)263-5326
Reproductions of traditional stands for antique trays, platters, lap desks, and boxes to be used as coffee and side tables. (R) (T)

SMITH & WATSON
The Decorative Arts Center
305 East 63rd St.
New York, N.Y. 10021
(212)355-5615

Available also at Ernest Gaspard & Associates, Atlanta; Kaplan & Fox, Inc., Boston; Patterson, Flynn & Martin, Chicago; John Edward Hughes, Inc., Dallas and Houston; Lawrence & Scott, Los Angeles; Hinkley & Associates, Inc., Philadelphia; and McCune, San Francisco.
Chairs, sofas, tables, breakfronts, chests, and desks; decorative replicas and adaptations of styles from Queen Anne to Regency; Chesterfield sofas, mirrors, lamps, executive desks, credenzas, and children's chairs. (T)

FREDERICK P. VICTORIA & SON, INC.
154 East 55th St.
New York, N.Y. 10022
(212)755-2549
Handmade facsimile reproductions of 18th-century English furniture, including chairs, breakfronts, mirrors; antique furniture. (R) (W)

AD HOC SOFTWARES
410 West Broadway
New York, N.Y. 10012
(212)925-2652
Cotton flannel sheets, woolen blankets, mohair throws, rag rugs, looped cotton bath mats. (R) (W)

AGATHA'S COZY CORNER
Woodbury Plaza
Portsmouth, N.H. 03801
(603)436-0102
Cotton flannel sheets, pillowcases, and duvet covers in prints and solids; cotton chenille bedcovers, cotton twill and thermal blankets, knitted cotton throws; all wool horse rugs; goose-down duvets. (MO)

LAURA ASHLEY
714 Madison Ave.
New York, N.Y. 10021
(212)371-0099
and 55 stores across the United States. Call 1-800-367-2000 for information about stores and for mail-order kits of current collection.
Coordinating fabrics, wall coverings, and borders in small geometrics, florals, and stripes; glazed chintzes in traditional designs; sheets, duvet covers, towels, table linens, rugs, patchwork quilts, and accessories; vinyl-coated and quilted fabrics; a special selection of vinyl wall coverings and cotton furnishings through decorators. (R) (MO)

HENRI BENDEL
10 West 57th St.
New York, N.Y. 10019
(212)247-1100
Table mats and napkins at Frank McIntosh shop; mohair throws, striped cotton sheets, embroidered

blanket covers, and pillow shams at Jane Wilmer shop. (R)

BRADBURY & BRADBURY WALLPAPERS
P.O. Box 155
Benicia, Calif. 94510
(707)746-1900
Hand-printed wallpapers and borders in the Victorian style with designs by William Morris, Christopher Dresser, and August Pugin. (MO)

BRUNSCHWIG & FILS, INC.
979 Third Ave.
New York, N.Y. 10022
(212)838-7878

Showrooms also in Atlanta; Chicago; Dallas; Los Angeles; Miami; and Washington, D.C.; and available at E. Wells McLean, Boston; Regency Hour, Denver; and San Francisco; Ellouise Abbot Showroom, Houston; A. F. Brown, Philadelphia; Designers Showroom, Seattle; and E. D. Navarra, Troy, Michigan.
Woven fabrics, chintzes, and wall coverings from documentary designs, including The Royal Pavilion at Brighton Collection. (T)

CHERCHEZ
864 Lexington Ave.
New York, N.Y. 10021
(212)737-8215
Antique table and bed linens, paisley throws, needlepoint pillows, and samplers. (R)

CLARENCE HOUSE
40 East 57th St.
New York, N.Y. 10022
(212)752-2890
moving to 211 East 58th St early 1985.
(same telephone)

Showrooms also in Atlanta, Boston, Chicago, Dallas, Denver, Houston, Los Angeles, Miami, Philadelphia, Portland, and San Francisco.
Fabrics, wallpapers, and trimmings; hand-blocked document chintzes;

Antique table and bed linens, Cherchez

striéd, spattered, and grained wallpapers and borders; exclusive imports from England (T)

COLLIER-CAMPBELL LTD. DESIGNS FOR MARTEX
West Point Pepperell
1221 Ave. of the Americas
New York, N.Y. 10020
Available at major department stores. Call (212)382-5376 for information.
Bed linens and towels designed by Susan Collier and Sarah Campbell.

FURNISHING FABRICS P. KAUFMANN FABRICS
261 5th Ave.
New York, N.Y. 10016 USA
(212)686-6470

WALL COVERINGS FROM MANUSCREENS
20 Horizon Blvd.
So. Hackensack, N.J. 07606
(201)440-7000

CONRAN'S
160 East 54th St.
New York, N.Y. 10022
(212)371-2225

See Conran's listing under Contemporary Furniture for

other stores.
Coordinating fabrics and wall coverings; sheets, duvet covers, and table linens; coir matting by the yard, dhurrie rugs, and oversized pillows. (R) (MO)

COWTAN & TOUT
979 Third Ave.
New York, N.Y. 10022
(212)753-4488

Available also at Travis & Company, Atlanta; Devon Service, Boston; Rozmallir, Chicago and Troy, Michigan; John Edward Hughes, Dallas and Houston; Kneebler-Franchere, Denver, Los Angeles, San Francisco, and Seattle; and Joseph B. Croce, Philadelphia.
Chintzes in florals, stripes, and striés with coordinating wall coverings; some hand-blocked document designs; paisleys printed on wool, cotton, silk, and linen. (T)

ROSE CUMMING, INC.
232 East 59th St.
New York, N.Y. 10022
(212)758-0844

Showrooms also in Atlanta,

Boston, Chicago, Dallas, Denver, Houston, Los Angeles, San Francisco, and Washington, D.C.
English chintzes of unusual colorings in original and documentary designs; fine trimmings; antique furniture and accessories. (T)

DAN RIVER INC.
111 West 40th St.
New York, N.Y. 10018

Terence Conran's Millenium Collection™ of bed linens and towels available from major U.S. department stores.

FONTHILL LTD.
979 Third Ave.
New York, N.Y. 10022
(212)924-3000
Marbelized and striéd chintzes and wallpapers; hand-blocked document design chintzes. (T)

JEAN HOFFMAN-JANA STARR ANTIQUES
236 East 80th St.
New York, N.Y. 10028
(212)535-6930
Antique bed and table linens and laces; woven bedcovers, pillows, and lace panels. (R)

RALPH LAUREN HOME COLLECTION
1185 Ave. of the Americas
New York, N.Y. 10020
(212)930-2382
At major department stores.
Pure linen sheets and pillowcases in bright colors; solid and striped Oxford cotton bedding, sheets, and pillowcases in soft florals, tattersal checks, and plaids, all with coordinating bedspreads, throws, shams, and bed skirts; towels, shower curtains, and bath rugs; table linens, place mats, and napkins with coordinating tableware, including china, flatwear, stemware, brass accessories, and plastic glasses; wall coverings and fabric by the yard. (W)

LEE JOFA, INC.
979 Third Ave.
New York, N.Y. 10022
(212)889-3900

Showrooms also in Atlanta,
Boston, Chicago, Dallas, Los
Angeles, Miami, Philadelphia,
San Francisco, and
Washington, D.C.
*English cotton and linen prints,
hand-blocked chintzes, Jacobean
prints, damasks, horsehairs, laces,
and wall coverings; marbelized
wallpapers and chintzes.* (T)

LIBERTY OF LONDON
SHOPS, INC.
229 East 60th St.
New York, N.Y. 10022
(212)888-1057

Suburban Square
61 St. James Pl.
Ardmore, Pa. 19003
(215)649-0813

Water Tower
845 North Michigan Ave. Store
702
Chicago, Ill. 60611
(312)280-1134

56 Highland Park Village
Dallas, Tex. 75205
(214)528-1380

Furnishings distributed on
West Coast by Pindler &
Pindler. Call (213)970-0075 for
information about West Coast
and (212)391-2150 for general
information.
*Liberty floral prints on fine Tana
lawn cotton; several fabrics in
William Morris and Art Nouveau
designs; highly glazed chintzes in
traditional designs; sheets and
duvet covers.* (R) (T)

SCALAMANDRE
850 Third Ave.
New York, N.Y. 10022
(212)361-8500

Showrooms also in Atlanta,
Boston, Chicago, Dallas,
Houston, Los Angeles, Miami,
Philadelphia, and San
Francisco, and representatives
in other cities.

Garden furniture and tools, Zona

---

*Velvets, silks, damasks, printed
cottons, and wall coverings; several
document designs by William
Morris in fabrics and wallpapers.*(T)

CHRISTIAN
SCHLUMBERGER
1270 Third Ave.
New York, N.Y. 10021
(212)879-5530
*Chintzes, paisleys, stripes, and
woven fabrics, including cottons by
Designer's Guild.* (R) (T)

D. D. TILLETT
170 East 80th St.
New York, N.Y. 10021
(212)737-7313
*Custom designs hand-printed on
cotton sailcloth, batiste, and chintz;
patterns include stripes, florals,
and geometrics.* (R) (T)

GARDEN
FURNISHINGS

CHINA & GARDEN
THE GREENHOUSE CENTER
257 Main St.
Chatham, N.J. 07928
(201)635-8996

1 Snow Rd.
Marshfield, Mass. 02050
(617)834-9306
*Importer of red cedar
conservatories from England;
octagonal and rectangular
modular units with Victorian
detailing; freestanding and lean-to
models available; gazebos and
swimming pool covers.* (R) (MO)

CONRAN'S
160 East 54th St.
New York, N.Y. 10022
(212)371-2225

See Conran's listing under
Contemporary Furniture for
other stores.
*Deck chairs, garden umbrellas, and
folding park chairs and tables;
metal outdoor plant stands, garden
tools, and planters.* (R) (MO)

COUNTRY CASUAL
17317 Germantown Rd.
Germantown, Md. 20874
(301)428-3434
*Teak garden seats, benches, and
tables in Chippendale, Warwick,
Mendip, and Severn designs;
English garden tools.* (R) (MO)

DESIGN HOUSE
425 Fifth Ave.
New York, N.Y. 10016
(212)889-0983

Playhouse Square
Westport, Conn. 06880
(203)227-2967
Latticework gazebo in kit form. (R)

FLORILEGIUM
Box 157
Sneden's Landing
Palisades, N.Y. 10964
(914)359-2926
*Antique botanical, bird, landscape,
and animal prints.* (MO)

GARDENS
1818 West 35th
Austin, Tex. 78703
(512)451-5490
*English willow garden trugs; teak
furniture, including Lutyens
bench; tools and books.* (R)

MACHIN DESIGNS (U.S.A.),
INC.
P.O. Box 167
Rowayton, Conn. 06853
(203)853-9983
*Ornamental garden houses and
conservatories imported from
England; trellished gazebos, summer
houses, and conservatories with
vaulted ceilings in free standing and
lean-to versions for use as house
extensions, swimming pool covers, and
greenhouses.* (MO)

TIMOTHY MAWSON
134 West 92nd St.
New York, N.Y. 10025
(212)874-6839
*Rare, out-of-print, and new books
on gardens and flowers, garden
history, landscape architecture,
botanical art, and English life. By
appointment only.* (MO)

THE CLAPPER COMPANY
1121 Washington St.
West Newton, Mass. 02165
(617)244-7900
*Teak garden benches, chairs,
tables, and chaises; English garden
tools and planters; gardening
books.* (R) (T) (MO)

THE WATER MILL
Watermill, N.Y. 11976
(516)726-4400
Teak garden benches, chairs, and tables. (R)

VINTAGE WOOD WORKS
P.O. Box 1157
Fredericksburg, Tex. 78624
(512)997-9513
Victorian wooden gazebo in kit form. (MO)

ZONA
484 Broome St.
New York, N.Y. 10013
(212)925-6750
English teak garden furniture; contemporary twig and New Mexican Mission furniture; English gardening tools, willow trugs, and terra-cotta planters. (R)

HARDWARE AND ARCHITECTURAL ELEMENTS

ARCHITECTURAL PANELING, INC.
979 Third Ave.
New York, N.Y. 10022
(212)371-9632
Hand-carved mantels, fireplaces, wall paneling; carved wooden moldings. (T)

ARTISTIC BRASS
4100 Ardmore Ave.
South Gate, Calif. 90280
(213)564-1100
Brass bathroom hardware with porcelain, wood, and Wedgwood detailing. (W)

BALL AND BALL
463 West Lincoln Hwy.
Exton, Pa. 19341
(213)363-7330
Cabinet hardware, door knockers, and fireplace accessories. (R) (MO)

THE DECORATIVE HARDWARE STUDIO
160 King St.

Architectural artifacts and sinks, Great American Salvage Co.

Chappaqua, N.Y. 10514
(914)238-5220
Hardware, including brass and porcelain bathroom faucets, campaign-style furniture hardware, and brass moldings; brass carpet rods. (R) (T)

DESIGNER RESOURCE
5160 Melrose Ave.
Los Angeles, Calif. 90038
(213)465-9235
Architectural elements, including columns, capitals, friezes, moldings, and mantels. (R) (T)

FOCAL POINT, INC.
2005 Marietta Rd., N.W.
Atlanta, Ga. 30318
(404)351-0820
Architectural ornamentation, including moldings, niches, domes, and mantels reproduced in plastic.

GREAT AMERICAN SALVAGE CO.
34 Cooper Square
New York, N.Y. 10003
(212)505-0070

3 Main St., Montpelier, Vt. 05602
(802)223-7711
Antique architectural building materials and artifacts, including

stained glass, doors, mantels, columns, lighting fixtures, pedestal sinks, bars, pharmacy cabinets, and bathroom fixtures. (R) (T)

P. E. GUERIN, INC.
23 Jane St.
New York, N.Y. 10014
(212)243-5270
Brass bathroom and cabinet hardware in traditional styles. (R)

THE HEARTHSTONE
2711 East Coast Hwy.
Corona del Mar, Calif. 92625
(714)673-7065
Fireplace tools, grates, and accessories in brass, steel, and chrome; antique fenders; custom-made door screens. (R) (T)

HORTON BRASSES
P.O. Box 95, Nooks Hill Rd.
Cromewell, Conn. 06416
(203)635-4400
Brass cabinet hardware in Hepplewhite, Sheraton, Queen Anne, Chippendale, and Victorian styles. (MO)

PUTNAM ROLLING LADDER CO.
32 Howard St.
New York, N.Y. 10013

(212)226-5147
Rolling library ladders in oak, made to order. (R) (W)

THE RENOVATOR'S SUPPLY, INC.
Millers Falls, Mass. 01349
(413)659-3163
Bathroom fixtures in brass, porcelain, and oak, including wooden toilet seats; rolling library ladders, cabinet hardware, and glass lampshades. (MO)

THE WRECKING BAR, INC.
2601 McKinney
Dallas, Tex. 75204
(214)826-1717
Architectural paneling, doors, mantels, stairways; fire grates; lighting fixtures. (R) (T)

HOUSEWARES

ASPREY
Trump Tower, 725 Fifth Ave.
New York, N.Y. 10022
(212)688-1811
Fine cutlery and silverware; outfitted wicker picnic hampers; bar and smoking accessories. (R)

BARNEY'S CHELSEA PASSAGE
Barneys
106 Seventh Ave.
New York, N.Y. 10011
(212)929-9000
Outfitted picinc hampers; flatware; candlesticks; glass and china; and table linens. (R)

HENRI BENDEL
10 West 57th St.
New York, N.Y. 10019
(212)247-1100
David Mellor flatware, horn-handled cutlery, nutcrackers, ceramics, trays, and hand-blown glass by Simon Pearce at Frank McIntosh shop; earthenware platters and bowls, teakettles, plastic-handled cutlery at Lee Bailey shop. (R)

CONRAN'S
160 East 54th St.
New York, N.Y. 10022
(212)371-2225

See Conran's listing under
Contemporary Furniture for
other stores.
*English ironstone dinnerware,
teapots, toast racks, pine and tin
trays, glassware, flatware, china
mixing bowls, dish drainers and
housewares, picnicware, table
linens, and kitchen towels.* (R) (MO)

CRATE AND BARREL
850 N. Michigan Ave.
Chicago, Ill. 60611
(312)787-5900

48 Brattle St.
Cambridge, Mass. 02138
(617)876-6300

Stores also in Boston, suburban
Chicago, and Dallas

Mail order only:
190 Northfield Rd.
Northfield, Ill. 60093
*Contemporary housewares,
including teapots, canisters, kettles,
glassware, and Hornsea Concept
dinnerware.* (R) (MO)

DEAN & DELUCA
121 Prince St.
New York, N.Y. 10012
(212)431-1691

46 Newton Lane
East Hampton, N.Y. 11937
(516)324-5790
*Smithfield ham pedestals,
stoneware baking dishes and mugs,
pudding basins, mixing bowls,
silver-plated marrow spoons,
cookware, and bakeware.* (R)

KITCHEN BAZAAR
4455 Connecticut Ave. N.W.
Washington, D.C. 20008
(202)363-4600

Stores also in Maryland and
Virginia.
*Imported teapots, electric kettles, and
English ceramic cookware.* (R) (MO)

LA CUISINIERE, INC.

Cookware and bakeware, Dean & DeLuca

687 Madison Ave.
New York, N.Y. 10021
(212)861-4475
*Antique and modern dessert plates,
platters, pâté molds, cookware,
majolica, and glassware.* (R)

JENNY B. GOODE, INC.
1194 Lexington Ave.
New York, N.Y. 10028
(212)794-2492
*Art Deco metal teapots and kettles,
Carltonware china, fruit plates,
and nurseryware.* (R)

GUMP'S
250 Post St.
San Francisco, Calif. 94108
(415)982-1616

Stores also in Beverly Hills,
Dallas, and Houston
*Fine English china, crystal, and
silver; large collection of antique
silver.* (R)

DOUGLAS LORIE
234 Worth Ave.
Palm Beach, Fla. 33480
(305)655-0700
*Fine antique English silver; some
reproduction sterling silver
flatware, tea services, candlesticks,
and serving pieces.* (R)

DAVID ORGELL
320 North Rodeo Dr.
Los Angeles, Calif. 90210
(213)272-3355
*Antique and reproduction silver,
including serving pieces,
candlesticks, and tea and coffee
services; flatware.* (R)

POTTERY BARN
231 10th Ave.
New York, N.Y. 10011
(212)741-9120

Stores also throughout New
York City and in Hartford,
Conn.; Manhasset, N.Y.;
Scarsdale, N.Y.; and Stamford,
Conn.
*Ironstone dinner sets, flatware,
teapots, kettles, gadgets, and
glassware.* (R)

JAMES ROBINSON, INC.
15 East 57th St.
New York, N.Y. 10022
(212)752-6166
*Handmade sterling silver flatware
available in 18 patterns.* (R) (T)

SHREVE, CRUMP AND LOW
330 Boylston St.
Boston, Mass. 02116
(617)267-9100

*Contemporary and antique silver
flatware, porcelain, china, glass,
and decorative accessories.* (R)

TIFFANY & CO.
727 Fifth Ave.
New York, N.Y. 10022
(212)755-8000

Stores also in Atlanta, Beverly
Hills, Chicago, Dallas,
Houston, Kansas City, and San
Francisco.
*All major lines of English bone
china and ironstone; two exclusive
designs in earthenware by Susie
Cooper; cut crystal; sterling silver
flatware, tea services, salvers,
candlesticks, and a variety of
hollowware; English carriage
clocks and chronometers.* (R)

WEDGWOOD
304 Stockton St.
San Francisco, Calif. 94108
(415)391-5610

Galleria, Suite 3745
5085 Westheimer
Houston, Tex. 77156
(713)627-0642
*Wedgwood's own stores, carrying
the complete line of all the china
designs.* (R)

WILLIAMS-SONOMA
576 Sutter St.
San Francisco, Calif. 94102

Mail order only:
P.O. Box 7456
San Francisco, Calif. 94120

Stores also in Costa Mesa,
Calif.; Dallas; Denver; Los
Angeles; Minneapolis; Palo
Alto; San Francisco; Short
Hills, N.J.; and Stamford,
Conn.
*Teapots, electric kettles, embossed
fruit plates, sugar sifters,
strawberry bowls, cotton and linen
kitchen towels, picnicware, and
bakeware.* (R) (MO)